In Search of Health Care Compliance 2001

Roy J. Snell, MHA, CHC
Senior Manager
PricewaterhouseCoopers, LLP
Minneapolis, Minnesota

Debbie Troklus, CHC
Assistant Vice President of Compliance
University of Louisville
Louisville, Kentucky

AN ASPEN PUBLICATION®
Aspen Publishers, Inc.
Gaithersburg, Maryland
2001

Library of Congress Cataloging-in-Publication Data

Snell, Roy J.
In search of health care compliance 2001/Roy J. Snell, Debbie Troklus
p. cm.
Includes index
ISBN 0-8342-1927-1 (alk. paper)
1. Health facilities—Law and legislation—United States.
2. Medical care—Law and legislation—United States.
3. Insurance, Health—Law and legislation—United States.
4. Medicare fraud—Prevention
KF3825.Z9 S64 2000
344.73'0321 dc—21
00-049333

Copyright © 2001 by Aspen Publishers, Inc.
A Wolters Kluwer Company
www.aspenpublishers.com
All rights reserved.

Aspen Publishers, Inc., grants permission for photocopying for limited personal or internal use. This consent does not extend to other kinds of copying, such as copying for general distribution, for advertising or promotional purposes, for creating new collective works, or for resale. For information, address Aspen Publishers, Inc., Permissions Department, 200 Orchard Ridge Drive, Suite 200, Gaithersburg, Maryland 20878.

Orders: (800) 638-8437
Customer Service: (800) 234-1660

About Aspen Publishers • For more than 40 years, Aspen has been a leading professional publisher in a variety of disciplines. Aspen's vast information resources are available in both print and electronic formats. We are committed to providing the highest quality information available in the most appropriate format for our customers. Visit Aspen's Internet site for more information resources, directories, articles, and a searchable version of Aspen's full catalog, including the most recent publications: **www.aspenpublishers.com**
  Aspen Publishers, Inc. • The hallmark of quality in publishing
  Member of the worldwide Wolters Kluwer group.

Editorial Services: Timothy Sniffin
Library of Congress Catalog Card Number: 00-049333
ISBN: 0-8342-1927-1

Printed in the United States of America

Dedication

I would like to thank Marc Dettmann and Dr. Scott Springmann, who helped me and the health care compliance industry. They and others at the University of Wisconsin dedicated much of their time and money to help facilitate the development of this industry through their support of the Health Care Compliance Association and several compliance-related publications.

—Roy J. Snell

I would like to thank several of my colleagues at the University of Louisville, especially Dr. Robert Slaton, who personally asked me to get into this field even though I was very reluctant; Dr. Al Thompson, who worked with me to initiate the compliance program at a time when there was not a lot of information available to help us; Dr. Joel Kaplan, dean of the Medical School, for his ongoing support and commitment; and Dr. Mark Pfeifer, my boss and dear friend, who gives me independence to make decisions and advice when I ask. I would also like to dedicate this book in memory of R. Thomas Carter, Esq., who provided counsel and guidance to us in the design of our initial compliance program.

—Debbie Troklus

The views and opinions in the following chapters are those of the individuals interviewed and do not necessarily reflect the views and opinions of their employers.

Contents

Foreword vii

Preface ix

Interview 1—Lewis Morris 1
    Office of Inspector General,
    U.S. Department of Health and Human Services

Interview 2—William M. Altman 17
    Vencor, Inc.

Interview 3—F. Lisa Murtha 31
    KPMG

Interview 4—Joe Beck 43
    Quorum Health Resources, LLC

Interview 5—Sue Prophet 53
    American Health Information Management
    Association

Interview 6—L. Stephen Vincze 63
    Vincze & Frazer, LLC

Interview 7—Sheryl Vacca 83
        Sutter Health

Interview 8—Odell Guyton 95
        University of Pennsylvania

Interview 9—John Steiner 101
        Cleveland Clinic Health System

Interview 10—Michael C. Hemsley 111
        Catholic Health East

Interview 11—Rob Sevell 127
        Foley & Lardner

Interview 12—Alan Yuspeh 135
        HCA—The Healthcare Company

Interview 13—Peter Grant 143
        Davis Wright Tremaine

Interview 14—Robert Dondero 149
        PricewaterhouseCoopers, LLP

Interview 15—Eugene Porter 157
        Montefiore Medical Center

Interview 16—Albert Bothe, Jr. 167
        University of Chicago

Index 175

Foreword

The field of corporate compliance has undergone significant growth and change over the past six years or so as the result of the expanding reach of enforcement efforts by both the federal and state governments. The Department of Justice (DOJ), Department of Health and Human Services Office of Inspector General (OIG), Federal Bureau of Investigation (FBI), and State Medicaid Fraud Control Units (MFCUs) have engaged in large and small, national and local, and criminal and civil investigations and prosecutions at an unprecedented rate. A high-ranking enforcement official once told me that in his almost twenty years of government service he had never seen the enforcement community gear up to take on one issue as they have for health care fraud. Out of these unprecedented initiatives corporate compliance programs for health care organizations were born. The only question is if these enforcement initiatives will be the driving force that will sustain our programs.

It is an exciting time to be involved in health care corporate compliance. It is not often that you get the chance to be at the forefront of a new profession. Today you would be hard-pressed to find a health care organization that does not have a compliance program. In fact, a recent Health Care Compliance Association (HCCA) survey showed that close to 96 percent of all health care organizations have a compliance program in place or under development. Contrast this fact with the notion that just a short six years ago, when I was the compliance officer at Thomas Jefferson University and Health System, I could count the number of compliance officers in health care on my hands. Now that the health care industry has embraced compliance programs as a necessity in order to make prosecutors less anxious and prevent fraud from occurring within their organizations, what will our future hold?

If the enforcement machine were to be turned off tomorrow, should the chief executive and board of directors of your organization still approve your expanding budget? The answer to this question needs to be "yes" if we are to make compliance departments a real necessity in health care. To do this, we need to ensure that compliance programs are not merely a preventative mechanism designed to prevent billing errors from becoming false claims, but rather that compliance programs lead to good business practices and better business practices lead to better, more efficient organizations.

Much has been written about the legal benefits of compliance programs, but what about the business benefits? We know that compliance programs lead to stronger controls within an organization and that stronger controls lead to better, more efficient organizations. As an industry, however, we need to start promoting these business benefits of our programs. No longer can a compliance department be recognized as an internal police squad. Rather, the compliance department should become known as the group that promotes efficiency and effectiveness within the operations of your organization.

Every compliance professional, in every compliance department, needs to confront the future reality of their field. One day, we will wake up, open the newspaper, and read that the war against health care fraud and abuse is over. When that time comes, even if it is not for several years, we all need to be prepared to demonstrate the "business" reasons for keeping our programs and departments intact. This should not be difficult to accomplish if we stop looking at only "billing errors" and start looking for ways to improve our operations.

It is in recognizing the future of compliance programs that the importance of *In Search of Health Care Compliance 2001* becomes clear. This book contains interviews with leading professionals in the field of corporate compliance in health care. To ensure the long-term viability of compliance programs, we will need to continue to learn from and share ideas with each other. I commend Roy J. Snell, Debbie Troklus, and the contributors to this book who are committed to furthering our profession by openly sharing ideas and practices with us all.

Brent L. Saunders, JD, MBA
Director
PricewaterhouseCoopers, LLP
Washington, DC

Preface

What is compliance? Compliance is a term that has many definitions that all point to a single, simple thought—compliance leads to doing the right thing. Yet, while compliance programs make good business sense and provide numerous benefits, people still question their need.

In Search of Health Care Compliance 2001 helps us drill down to the core of compliance to determine what it really means by presenting a compilation of thoughts from a diverse group of compliance professionals. The individuals interviewed in this book have backgrounds in education, audit, law, reimbursement, patient care, regulatory, and administrative areas. They come from all aspects of health care such as group practice, nursing home, hospital, and other related segments of health care. They come from all sizes of organizations—from small hospitals to large academic institutions—and represent various roles, such as in-house counsel, compliance officers, auditors, physicians, chief executive officers (CEOs), and consultants.

These individuals strive to answer questions about several topics, from the fundamentals of compliance to complex and as yet unresolved definitions of the roles and responsibilities of compliance programs. They share solutions they have used to resolve complex compliance issues, speculate on the future and analyze the past, and offer a wide range of sometimes controversial solutions and analysis.

Health care compliance is complicated, young, and fraught with peril and confusion. The challenges associated with understanding all of the regulations, assessing organizations' compliance with those regulations, and convincing leadership to fix problems aggressively are staggering.

Five years ago the health care compliance industry exploded onto the scene. We are still working to define what is inside the box and what is outside the box. The individuals involved in this book help us further define and resolve these challenges.

Great effort and time went into the development of this book. We thank all of the participants for their time and ideas. Their efforts will help many individuals who often struggle with these issues.

Interview 1

Lewis Morris

Assistant Inspector General for Legal Affairs
Office of Inspector General
U.S. Department of Health and Human Services

Mr. Morris spearheads the Office of Inspector General's (OIG) efforts in health care enforcement. Dedicated to helping the health care industry improve its systems and procedures, he candidly shares his perspective on many issues regarding OIG enforcement activities and related compliance issues.

Snell and Troklus: What exactly is your position with the Department of Health and Human Services, and what are your main responsibilities?

Morris: I am the assistant inspector general for legal affairs within the Office of Inspector General. As such, I and Mac Thornton, the chief counsel, share responsibility for oversight of the staff of over seventy attorneys and paralegals. Our primary function is to serve our client, the inspector general [IG], which means we have a wide range of legal duties. We are responsible for general advisory functions that you would expect from any legal office. We also represent the Office of Inspector General in litigation, both defensive litigation in the area of employment and personnel work, and proactive litigation against those who have defrauded our program and against whom we are pursuing administrative sanctions. In addition, our staff provides everything from advisory opinions to compliance guidances to negotiating corporate integrity agreements for matters relating to the False Claims Act. We are a wide-ranging legal office with a heavy specialty in health care fraud and authorities under the Inspector General's Act.

Source: Copyright © 2000, Lewis Morris, JD.

Snell and Troklus: Have you been instrumental in the design of any of the Office of Inspector General guidances?

Morris: Ultimately, I am responsible for the work of my staff. I would have to say, first and foremost, that all of the staff are fabulous. There are certain members of the staff who are just outstanding, such as Larry Goldberg, the branch chief in the Civil Recoveries Branch, who has overseen the creation of the compliance guidances. It is his staff who writes the guidances. He personally edits and reedits every one of them so that they are in conformance with our practices and so that every sentence can withstand scrutiny. While I may get all the credit for the guidances, folks like Larry Goldberg really do the work. Because of the axiom about walking a mile in someone else's moccasins, I personally wrote the nursing home guidance so that I would have a better understanding of what goes into writing one. So I have had direct involvement with one, and I oversee and edit all of them.

Snell and Troklus: What is the process used in their design? I know you have a concept, and then you move forward. What are the steps to finalization?

Morris: The first step is deciding which industry sectors we should devote our time and energy to, and that in large part comes from looking at the prior enforcement history of that industry sector. It is not surprising that the first place we began was the independent clinical labs, because we just finished settling False Claims Act cases with the clinical labs in excess of $800 million in liability. We thought they might use a little guidance on how to avoid future problems. Our next guidance was directed to hospitals, in light of all the work we do in the enforcement arena with hospitals. So part of the process is deciding which industry sector appears to need guidance based on enforcement experience.

We then look at the types of cases that have been brought to court in that industry and the sorts of audits, evaluations, and inspections we have done to form the structure of the risk areas. If you look at the guidances, in many ways they are very similar. They all track the seven elements of the U.S. Sentencing Commission. They all recommend, for example, adequate training of support staff, and they all suggest codes of conduct. The area in the guidance that takes the most work and requires the most tailoring is the risks to be addressed as part of the policies and procedures.

The next step is to determine which risk areas should be addressed, prioritize those, and then come up with practical ways to identify and respond to those risks. Once we have the concepts and basic structure in place, we go out to the affected provider community and ask for its suggestions. We do that through the *Federal Register* to ensure a wider opportunity for input. We then take all those comments, read every one of them many times, and add those suggestions to our outline. Several months later, we have a draft product, which we share with the Department of Justice [DOJ] and the Health Care Financing Administration [HCFA] as our two primary partners. We get their comments, and then the document is rewritten again and sent out for public comments. So we get the industry's input yet a second time. Once those comments are assimilated, we once again give the draft back to HCFA and DOJ. We also reach out to the other inspector generals so that they can have input, since we try to make the guidance relevant not only to Medicare/Medicaid, but to all the federal health care programs. After all that input is absorbed, often the DOJ wants yet another look at the draft guidance in case someone made a change of which they are not aware. Once all that input has been collected and has been reviewed by our staff, we submit it to the inspector general for her consideration and suggestions and to the other components of the IG to make sure that we are on track. Then it is finally published.

Snell and Troklus: I know now that you are working on the physician guidance. Do you see other guidances being released in the future?

Morris: The next one that would be a possibility is ambulance transport. That is an area where we have had a fair amount of enforcement history. There are specific risk areas that we can identify which we think an effective compliance program can address. After that, I think we probably hit all of the key health care sectors. As we say to the provider community in general, "If there are sectors that we think could benefit from a unique compliance guidance, we would be more than glad to consider it and get their suggestions." We are already seeing some overlap between the physician practice guide and the third-party billing guide. The clinical laboratory guide and the hospital guide have commonality in relation to in-house labs. We are beginning to see that positive overlap, which tells us that we are covering all the bases.

I think what we are likely to do, absent providers requesting additional guidances, is to give pause to creating new guidances. We will go back and

look at the earlier ones, such as lab, hospital, home health, and hospice, to see whether they need to be updated in light of what we have learned in the recent past and also to take into account changes in reimbursement. We had to say, "Thou shall unbundle all lab tests." So we have already revised the lab guidance once. I suspect that every one of the guidances has some aspect of risk area suggestions, particularly in billing, that needs to be reviewed again in light of programmatic changes.

Snell and Troklus: Coming from an academic setting, I hear a lot about research compliance. Do you think there will be an effort to provide guidance to the research arena?

Morris: I think that would be tremendous. The inspector general's office devotes a substantial part of its resources and budget to health care, in large part because HIPAA[1] is structured so that about 70 percent of our budget goes to protecting the health care trust funds. We have responsibility for ensuring the integrity of over 300 programs in the department, including

---

[1]Health Insurance Portality and Accountability Act

the National Institutes of Health [NIH] and thus all the research grants that are generated through that institution. I think it would be great if we had the skills, input, and cooperation of NIH to put together guidance for research. I know that NIH has been looking at that very thing. There have been a couple of False Claims Act settlements in which the equivalent of a corporate integrity agreement has been executed with the institution to ensure that the facilities maintain present responsibilities and are able to continue to participate as grantees. We would certainly welcome thought from within the government and from the research community about how to best construct a compliance guide, because I don't think we have the same depth of experience and knowledge in that area as we do in health care.

Snell and Troklus: What do you see is the future of Physicians at Teaching Hospitals [PATH]?

Morris: We have around 30 institutions that are at various stages of PATH reviews. Once those are completed, we will probably assess what we have learned in light of the changes in the teaching physician rules. We will probably take some time to see how those rules have been complied with. It is a pretty safe bet that at some point we will want to come back to see whether there is compliance under the new rules.

Snell and Troklus: Where do you see compliance programs in the next five years? Will they be as strong as they are today?

Morris: I would hope so, but there are a number of forces working at cross purposes. Compliance costs money; compliance officers necessarily are harbingers of bad news—telling your board of directors that there is an overpayment or a whistle blower—and they don't generally come in with great news about profits.

On the other side, you have a growing compliance industry, growing visibility, and we hope that the self-disclosure program will demonstrate that compliance officers can be part of getting problems resolved early and less expensively. You also have a growing risk from the plaintiff's bar that wants to sue providers, nursing homes, hospital chains, and the like. Hopefully compliance can be shown to protect against these lawsuits. Compliance programs are a little bit like a safety or passive restraint system: the only time you need it is when you just hit the brick wall. And until the moment you hit the wall, you don't know you need it. So there has to be some measure of faith that every day you buckle up because you never know when that wall is going to be around the corner. For skeptics who are wondering why they spent twenty-five bucks on a safety belt, you don't want to recommend that they slam into a wall to see that it works. In short, the compliance industry to some extent is hindered by the sentinel effect. You never can fully demonstrate the value of your service, because it's what didn't happen as a result of your work that is its greatest value. If an effective compliance program prevents a lawsuit from being filed or a criminal investigation from being opened, how do you measure that success?

I would like to believe that between HCCA,[2] the inspector general's initiatives, and the right thinking by boards of directors and CEOs who understand that compliance is not only the right thing to do but it makes good business sense, compliance programs will prosper in health care. I think one of the things we all have to do on the private side and the government side is make the case for compliance. Compliance is value-added service. There is a benefit to it. We really need to be thinking about ways to empirically demonstrate that compliance is a good investment. At some point, perhaps sooner than later, the economy is going to slow down, money is going to get tight, and people are going to start looking for ways to cut back. If you take a look at Medicare/Medicaid, the number of workers contributing to the program is going to drop over the next thirty years, while the number of beneficiaries is going to increase. There are three ways policy makers can address that coming reality. They can reduce benefits, reduce provider payments, or increase revenues. None of those choices is attractive. If you cut money to providers, the compliance program is going to be one place that providers will look to cut. I think all of us really need to build the empirical argument that this is a good investment. To answer your question, I think the future of compliance is promising but not without challenges.

Snell and Troklus: In your review of compliance programs across the country, do you feel that compliance budgets are adequate to do the job?

Morris: There is probably not enough money put into compliance. I don't know that is going to change radically, so what we ought to be doing as leaders

---

[2]Health Care Compliance Association

is coming up with more cost-effective ways to advance compliance. Collaboration between hospital groups on training, group practices sharing selected compliance functions, better use of technology, computer edits and screening instead of manual review on a postaudit basis—there are ways that we can help reduce the cost of compliance so that it is affordable. Yes, I agree there is probably not enough money put into budgets, but I am not sure the answer is spending more money on compliance. There are too many other competing demands for that dollar.

Snell and Troklus: Do you feel that inadequate budgets directly correspond to ineffective commitment from the top?

Morris: I suspect that sometimes inadequate budgets reflect a lack of resources, not a lack of commitment. When you think about small rural providers or others who have a very modest profit margin, they may make the assessment that it is more important to get a magnetic resonance imaging [MRI] machine into an area where there isn't one for another 500 miles than it is to pay for a compliance officer. I have to say that I don't disagree with that judgment. It comes back to how we can help those people who legitimately cannot afford a "gold-plated" compliance program understand that efforts on a smaller, less costly scale will still serve them well.

Snell and Troklus: We hear a lot about effective compliance programs. What steps should a compliance officer take to measure whether a compliance program is really effective?

Morris: By using outcome-based measures. In virtually all aspects of life, personal or professional, you can only tell if you are going forward by putting some sort of objective marker out there. Writing up a mission statement and coming back to it two years later, seeing whether you have met your goals or not. I think the way you tell whether you have an effective program is to put together some outcome-based measures that reflect where you would like to be. In the nursing home context, is your goal reduced incidence of decubitus ulcers and hydration problems? If so, get a marker on where everybody is now and aim to have fewer incidents as an objective in six months. On financial matters, the same rule applies. If you have an 18 percent error rate based on resubmitted claims to the Medicare program, have as an objective that in six months you are going to have an

11 percent error rate, and in a year and a half you're going to reduce it to 6 percent. Decide how you are going to measure that objective, and then start taking steps so that in six months you can see whether you made it. That's how you measure effectiveness. Although effectiveness may be in the eye of the beholder, there are objective ways of measuring it.

Snell and Troklus: Can you share an example of a case in which a health care organization did not follow its own policies and procedures, and you used the policy as evidence that the administrators did understand but didn't follow through with it?

Morris: I would not refer to a specific case by name, because, in all fairness, the vast majority of providers whom we investigate elect to settle with us and thus have not admitted any wrongdoing. While you can ask why anyone would pay $30 million when they didn't do anything wrong, it is reasonable not to accuse them of something to which they have not admitted. There are cases in which, based on our review of internal documents obtained through IG subpoena or other compulsory processes, we have identified an internal memorandum that clearly and correctly articulated the Medicare rule or standard. That kind of documentation obviously is very persuasive when we're rebutting a statement that the rules are vague and nobody can possibly understand them. I would say, as a general observation, that while some of our regulations can be difficult for the person on the street to understand, that is one of the reasons why HCFA hires contractors to help providers understand the rules.

Snell and Troklus: Are many health care organizations refusing to settle and demanding that the case go to court?

Morris: No, I think most large providers, such as hospitals, reputable home health agencies, and the like, can't afford the substantial legal costs. They can't afford the risk of losing and facing not only the full breadth of the False Claims Act, but also the risk of exclusion. Also, in many instances, they can't afford to have the truth come out. You can argue the nuances of a regulation to the government lawyer, and a teaching hospital can protest that it didn't understand what physical presence meant, but when a case is effectively presented to a jury by the government prosecutor, the ensuing publicity can be damaging.

The cases that get brought by DOJ and OIG are not based on obscure interpretations of the Medicare rules. Those who complain about "criminalizing innocent billing errors" (which is a remarkable mischaracterization of the law) fail to understand that prosecutors, by nature, are committed to the truth and like to win. They are not going to take cases that they have a probability of losing. If a jury cannot understand the theory of the government case, or if it appears to be based on arcane rules and that the government is at fault, there is going to be an acquittal. So the kinds of cases that are brought criminally, as well as civilly, are those where you can articulate your theory.

Snell and Troklus: What percentage of the cases end up in court as opposed to a settlement?

Morris: I don't have the numbers, but I would bet that well over 95 percent end up in settlement. Let me also stress that many allegations against health care providers are closed after an initial inquiry or are referred to the program for administrative handling. For example, the government intervenes in a fraction, about 20 percent, of all the *qui tams* that are filed in the health care area. The number of hotline calls we get is in the hundreds of thousands, and yet only a small fraction of those actually result in criminal prosecutions. I think we do an extremely effective job winnowing out the frivolous and the thinly based complaints and going after the real problems, because we have limited resources. I think that trade associations that complain that we are criminalizing innocent billing errors are simply wrong. We don't need to and can't afford to go after trivial mistakes when we have some huge fraud schemes taking place.

Snell and Troklus: How many corporate integrity agreements (CIAs) do you have in place?

Morris: Currently we have about 435. We have executed in total just over 500. Approximately 100 of them have expired. A large number will end in another year and a half or so, because our real bulge was in 1998, when a large number of hospitals entered into three-year CIAs as part of our national projects.

Snell and Troklus: How do you keep up with monitoring the corporate integrity agreements?

Morris: We have brought on extra staff, both lawyers and program analysts, to do that work. We did nine on-site inspections in 1999. We'll have a HCFA contractor do another 27 inspections, and we'll probably inspect another 18 providers ourselves. Those on-site inspections will verify that the information reported to us in the annual reports is consistent with actual conditions at the provider. We see these inspections as an opportunity to educate. We are not inclined to impose monetary penalties, exclusions, or any other sanctions for problems we may find. We want to make sure that providers under CIAs comply with our audit provisions. If they didn't, we give them a chance to do it again. We want to make this process work.

Unfortunately, we have identified a number of providers who have not honored the terms of their settlement agreements or CIAs, and so we already have imposed penalties and other stipulated sanctions on some providers.

Snell and Troklus: If an organization's CIA is getting ready to expire, and you find that there are still some deficiencies when you review them, can you extend their corporate integrity agreement?

Morris: No. The CIA is an agreement, a contract with a date of expiration, just like the lease on your car. Having said that, if we uncover a fraud scheme or substantial problems during the CIA review process or as part of an on-site review, we would obviously refer that matter to the OIG's Office of Investigations. If the allegations are substantiated, it is very likely we would see that provider under a new CIA, if it is not excluded again as part of the False Claims Act settlement.

Snell and Troklus: When you visit an organization to check its compliance with a CIA, can the organization inform its employees that you are coming and that they may be interviewed? In addition, can they tell their employees what you may be asking and inform the employees about the current state of the compliance program so that they can better answer the CIA review team's questions?

Morris: Yes. We see the visits as a way of keeping people on the right track. Preparing in advance is not unethical or illegal. We can't tell employers how or when to communicate with employees. But prepping employees brings us back to this issue of effectiveness. If you have to go tell your employees who the compliance officer is two weeks before our arrival, you probably have deeper problems; one way or another, these deficiencies in your compliance efforts will be manifest. We had an inspection on the west coast where the provider obviously prepared staff at the last minute. We spoke to the compliance officer and a randomly selected group of staff to find out how the compliance program was working. We asked three of the staff, "Who is your compliance officer?" and they didn't know. The compliance officer was sitting with them! Now, I suspect that they might have been introduced to the compliance officer prior to that meeting, but it went right over their heads.

So yes, you can go and tell people we're coming. You can make sure that your records are up to date, although you must not alter records, because we consider what we are doing an audit. There is a specific felony provision for obstructing a federal audit. It would be unwise to go back and re-create your hotline logs or other things that we will look at, but there is nothing wrong with explaining to your staff why we are going to be there and giving them the assurance that this is not part of some criminal investigation.

Snell and Troklus: What is the most consistent CIA compliance failure?

Morris: The problems or failures we encounter vary considerably. We probably have the greatest difficulties in the internal and independent review organization audits. I wouldn't call them failures, however, because in some cases our expectations in conducting the internal or external audits have been unclear. That is as much our fault as it is the fault of the counsel that negotiated the CIA with us. It is fair to say that in some of the instances where there has been a failure to conform to our audit protocols, it has been because of a lack of understanding of what we wanted.

Snell and Troklus: Would it help to have more communication throughout the course of the independent review organization's involvement than to wait for receipt of the report?

Morris: Yes, we are doing a number of things to address this issue. The first is to provide greater specificity in the corporate integrity agreement. This necessarily means that the corporate integrity agreement is longer. I think it is better to give more details so expectations can be met on the front end. We're also prepared, consistent with AICPA SOP 99–1, to review the agreed-upon procedures for the compliance assessment component of the

CIA. We also have posted a series of frequently asked questions on the OIG's web page on the Internet. However, it is also important that the compliance officer and independent review organization communicate with us. We have a staff of attorneys and program analysts whose job is to monitor the CIAs, so your compliance monitor in the OIG will be someone you can call to ask questions. Between personal contact, use of the Internet, and greater clarity in the agreement itself, I think we are on the way to addressing some of the confusion surrounding the role of the IRO.[3]

Snell and Troklus: If you see that an organization is not adequately complying with the terms of the corporate integrity agreement because of a single individual's negative attitude, lack of participation, and lack of support, is there anything you can do about it?

Morris: Ultimately, the organization chooses who will represent it. If you look at our settlement agreements and our corporate integrity agreements, we don't tell organizations who ought to be fired. But if you have a CEO who doesn't care about integrity or a regional manager who tries to circumvent the CIA or program rules, it is the organization that will bear the consequences of that individual's actions.

That said, we do focus on individuals; in fact, one of the OIG's priorities for the next couple of years is to put more of our energy into taking action against dishonest individuals. For example, in many instances we may not choose to exclude a nursing home because of the disruptive influence it will have on the residents of the home. However, we plan to devote substantial resources to developing the ability to go after administrators who oversee the delivery of poor care or who participate in fraud schemes. We have to hold individuals, particularly corporate leaders, responsible for their actions. But when it comes to failing to comply with a CIA or a company's failure to exercise control over its individuals, we are also going to hold the organization responsible.

Snell and Troklus: When you talk about holding people responsible, what is the compliance officer's liability? Would a compliance officer be held personally responsible for not finding a problem? Can he or she go to jail?

---

[3]independent review organization

Morris: In order to go to jail, you have to commit a crime. In order to commit a crime, you generally have to have specific intent. You can't inadvertently commit a health care violation and go to prison for it. Unless a compliance officer was complicit in and a party to criminal conduct, such as a coconspirator, I am hard-pressed to see any circumstance under which he or she would be held criminally liable.

Snell and Troklus: What if the compliance officer knew about something that was going on and did not do anything about it?

Morris: Under criminal law, if you actively aid and abet, actively assist in the commission of a crime, you can also be held liable. For example, if you know that a cost report is going to be turned in that contains false line items and you hide information that would bring the fraud to light, or you take other measures to obstruct the detection of that falsity after the fact, you can be implicated in the criminal conduct. People tend to overlook the fact that even after a crime has been committed, conduct such as destroying evidence, obstructing the investigation, or affirmatively misleading investigators or auditors can implicate people in addition to the initial wrongdoers. So, a compliance officer cannot go to jail for something he or she didn't know about. But a compliance officer can find himself or herself in a world of trouble for failing to use good judgment and allowing a criminal enterprise to continue.

Snell and Troklus: Will the number of corporate integrity agreements increase, decrease, or stay constant over the next twelve months, excluding the national program?

Morris: I think we have a pretty constant flow of CIAs because we have a pretty constant flow of False Claims Act cases. It is the nature rather than number of CIAs that will change. Although a parent company may have an effective compliance program when it acquires another company, it acquires new liabilities as well. Those liabilities result in a False Claims Act settlement, and we hold the parent company responsible. More and more companies are successfully arguing that they have a good program in place, so the CIA is increasingly tailored to the existing elements that work; then we supplement it. You may see a slight increase in CIAs because we continue to put more investigators, auditors, and prosecutors on line thanks to HIPAA. The real change will be in the content of the CIAs: they will be more detailed as to the IRO function, but some of them may not require IROs. There may be more specificity on training, but less in other areas, because the providers are able to demonstrate to us that they have effective compliance measures in place.

Snell and Troklus: Are the dollars recovered in settlements increasing, decreasing, or remaining flat?

Morris: They are increasing. Criminal convictions are certainly increasing: last year we had more than 300, whereas the year before we had a little under 200. False Claims Act cases, the source of the largest part of our civil recoveries, have also continued to rise quite substantially since the amendments in 1986. According to the Department of Justice, in 1987 we recovered less than $20 million, but in 1999 we recovered in excess of $300 million.

Snell and Troklus: What advice would you have for a compliance officer who meets resistance from administrators or physicians on conducting sanction checks on all administrators and physicians?

Morris: My advice would be to refer them to the federal regulations that allow us to impose civil monetary penalties on any individual or entity who employs or contracts with an excluded entity. The failure to make sure that you are hiring people who are not excluded can be very expensive.

Snell and Troklus: Half of the nursing home systems in the United States have filed for chapter 11 bankruptcy. Is this related to enforcement activities?

Morris: No, in my view this is related to a confluence of events, a significant one of which is the failure of these nursing home chains to anticipate that the Medicare program would move to a prospective payment system. The chains have also paid far too much for nursing homes, and they overleveraged themselves in order to exploit ancillary services in the therapy milieu. They found themselves with homes that had substantially overpriced leases and mortgages, and they had an inability to generate money through ancillary services to cover those costs. It's a matter of bad management. Those who complain that the Balanced Budget Act is the cause of this fail to note that Medicare represents around 10 percent of the revenues going into most nursing homes. It's hard to understand how, standing alone, a modification in the payment stream to 10 percent of your revenues could force you into bankruptcy. If a financial crisis was precipitated by the government, why is it that the boards of directors didn't address the compensation of executives in these now bankrupt nursing homes, some of whom have compensation that is just staggering? Some of these executives have interest-free loans, or no obligation to repay their loans, as well as golden parachutes of extraordinary depth. It seems to me that the problem here is bad management combined with other factors, not enforcement.

Snell and Troklus: Is the FBI's involvement in health care fraud and abuse cases increasing or decreasing, and why does the FBI get involved?

Morris: Their involvement is increasing, both because they are given money to do it and because it is a priority of the attorney general, second only to violent crime. It reflects a commitment from the administration as well as Congress to protect our seniors from the abuse that is weakening the long-term stability of the Medicare trust funds.

Snell and Troklus: The banking industry has a collaborative relationship with the enforcement community. How can we move health care in that direction?

Morris: I don't know a lot about the banking industry, except to say that I believe that the federal health care programs pale in comparison to that regulatory oversight. While the health care profession bridles at the level of regulation that exists now, if they were to look at the level that exists with banking regulators, the site visits by banking examiners and the like, they would probably object. I am not so sure that they are wrong. One of the real pluses of the Medicare program is great flexibility for local medical practice. The program is designed to give physicians the ability to practice the art of medicine within a limited regulatory environment. It would be unfortunate to impinge on that.

Interview 2

William M. Altman
Vencor, Inc.

William Altman is the vice president of compliance with publicly traded Vencor, Inc. He brings expertise from various aspects, such as hospitals, nursing homes, pharmacies, home health, and hospice.

Troklus: First of all, what is your background and how did you get interested in the field of compliance?

Altman: I am a licensed attorney and have practiced health care law for the past fifteen years in private and public sector settings. In addition, I have a master's degree in public health policy and have worked in a variety of policy-related settings. I suppose I have always practiced in the field of compliance. There is somewhat of a misunderstanding in the public policy community that compliance in health care is a new concept. In fact, health care providers and those advising health care providers have long implemented measures to ensure compliance with the complex set of regulations that govern provider operations. Although the formalization of health care compliance programs is a recent phenomenon, the concept of compliance is not new. As a practicing lawyer, I often found myself advising health care providers on how to structure their operations to minimize the liability associated with noncompliance. As a health care consultant, I not only helped providers interpret complex regulations, but also modified their operations to meet the regulations without compromising their operational objectives. That role best summarizes my interest in compliance: to help providers and regulators deliver health care in compliance with rules and regulations while at the same time supporting operations.

Troklus: Let's start by setting the stage. Tell me a little bit about Vencor's organizational structure.

Altman: Vencor is a provider of long-term care services with two major operating divisions. First, we have 300 nursing homes operating in about thirty-eight states. Second, we have fifty-eight long-term, acute-care hospitals providing services in approximately thirty states. We also provide rehabilitation services to our nursing home residents. We have thirty-seven institutional pharmacies, which provide pharmacy services to customer nursing homes. We have a corporate office with 800 employees in Louisville, Kentucky, and several regional offices distributed throughout the country in the operating divisions of both hospitals and nursing facilities. Obviously, our compliance program needs to be structured to respond to the compliance issues that arise in our different lines of business. In addition, we must structure the compliance program to reflect the organizational structure of the company itself.

Troklus: How long has Vencor's compliance program been in effect?

Altman: Vencor began structuring its compliance program approximately three years ago. We started, as most organizations do, by crafting a code of conduct, activating a compliance hotline, and implementing the various policies and procedures needed to ensure compliance with the fundamental laws that govern our activities. The most important indicator of an effective compliance program is one that, once adopted, is not cast in stone. It must change with the internal and external environments. Since Vencor first adopted its compliance program, there have been significant changes not only in the regulations, but also in the enforcement environment for long-term care. As a result, our compliance program has evolved to address those issues. For example, the reimbursement system for nursing facilities went from a retrospective, cost-based system to a prospective, fixed payment–based system. The compliance issues that arise under a cost-based system—namely, the concern that there is an overutilization of services, which results in unnecessarily high costs to the government—do not exist under a prospective reimbursement system. On the contrary, the major compliance issue under a prospective system is ensuring that underutilization does not occur. Our compliance program has had to adapt to these changes and to implement controls to address the dynamic nature of the environment.

Troklus: What are Vencor's current compliance initiatives?

Altman: At the time of this interview, many health care organizations, including Vencor, are in active negotiations with the Office of Inspector General [OIG]. As a result, the major compliance initiative for Vencor is the negotiation, implementation, and monitoring of a corporate integrity agreement. While many health care organizations view corporate integrity agreements as an unfortunate interference of the government into their operations, our perspective is different. We view the negotiation as an opportunity to engage in a constructive dialogue with the OIG, to define what its expectations are with respect to compliance in long-term care, and to determine how that can be best achieved.

The OIG, for its part, has taken this opportunity to understand in more detail the operational challenges faced by long-term care providers—including the challenges we all face with regard to staffing—and has structured the corporate integrity agreement to reflect those challenges. While there are many areas of disagreement, and plenty of opportunity for disagreements in the implementation of the corporate integrity agreement, I am optimistic that there is more potential for a public–private partnership in our corporate integrity agreement than might exist without it. It is my hope that both the health care compliance community and the government community will view these corporate integrity agreements as an opportunity for increased collaboration. That is what is most needed in health care compliance today.

Troklus: What is your opinion of the *Long-Term Care Model Compliance Guide* issued by the OIG?

Altman: In certain respects, the guide reflects some innovative thinking. For example, the OIG, for the first time, put in writing some of its preliminary thoughts on what constitutes an effective compliance program. However, beyond listing its seven attributes of an effective compliance program, the OIG has provided no further guidance on what constitutes an effective compliance program. I am hopeful that, by raising the issue in the compliance guide, the OIG is inviting more public discussion.

The compliance guidance for nursing facilities is unique in its focus on quality of care as a compliance issue. Many health care providers may disagree with the characterization of quality of care as a compliance issue. But the public nature of quality of care, particularly in long-term care, makes it inevitable that various government agencies that heretofore have not characterized quality as a compliance issue will do so in the future. Therefore, the health care provider community should embrace compliance as a quality issue and become active in defining the context in which quality of care is a compliance issue.

Having said that, I think the OIG guide does not provide much innovative thinking in how quality of care is a compliance issue, beyond listing the regulatory quality of care requirements and stating, in an outcome-oriented fashion, that providers should design measures to ensure compliance with those requirements. What would be more helpful is a constructive dialogue between researchers, public policy makers, operators, and clinicians. Focusing on best practices in quality of care and linking those practices with reimbursement policy would ensure that providers have the resources to furnish quality of care. At that point, they should be accountable

for the care that they provide. Again, I am hopeful that the OIG views the guidance as an introduction to quality of care as a compliance issue and as a first step in inviting a constructive dialogue on the issue. Whether that will be the case remains to be seen.

Troklus: Did issuance of the guidance affect the design of your program in any way?

Altman: No. Because of our extensive discussions with the OIG over the course of the past year on the development of a corporate integrity agreement, we had already begun to implement many aspects of the compliance guidance. On a professional note, however, the OIG's raising of the compliance program effectiveness issue has prompted me to engage in some public writing about that issue.

Troklus: What would you say are the top five billing problems you would look for in long-term care?

Altman: I would identify three major billing issues. First, with the advent of the prospective payment system [PPS] for Medicare services, the primary issue is the accuracy of the clinical assessments that are used to assign reimbursement categories under the Resource Utilization Group (RUG-III) system. Residents are classified into reimbursement categories based on the resources they will require to meet their care needs. The accuracy of the reimbursement claims submitted to the government rests on the accuracy of the underlying clinical assessment. Therefore, from a billing perspective and from a compliance perspective, it is important to ensure the accuracy of the underlying clinical assessment.

Second, while Medicare Part A claims are reimbursed under a prospective payment system, certain rehabilitation and other services are still reimbursed under a cost-based methodology for Medicare Part B claims. Therefore, various compliance issues regarding overutilization still exist.

Third, many nursing facilities receive a significant amount of reimbursement from the Medicaid program. While many state Medicaid programs are moving toward prospective, RUG-III–based reimbursement systems, many states still reimburse nursing facilities for care provided to Medicaid residents on a cost-based system. Cost-based reimbursement requires the filing of cost reports. Accordingly, the traditional compliance issues that arise under cost-based systems as well as the completion and filing of cost reports remain a concern for any subset of financial claims submitted by providers to the government.

Troklus: I've heard a lot recently about "RUGs creep." What exactly does it mean?

Altman: The term "RUGs creep" is a variant of the term "DRG creep," which was coined with the advent of the prospective payment system for hospitals, implemented in 1983. The government's concern is that the clinical assessments, which determine the reimbursement rates, can be manipulated to essentially overcode and can thus result in higher, inappropriate reimbursement for the nursing facility. Frankly, I think the government's concern here with respect to the prospective payment system for nursing facilities is overstated. Unlike the DRG[1] reimbursement system, many of the reimbursement categories for the RUG system are driven by the actual provision of services, which must be reflected in the clinical record. Therefore, manipulating the system to result in overcoding is much more difficult than the government would believe. Nevertheless, there are compliance issues lurking within any reimbursement system that rests on clinical assessments, and therefore some compliance controls are still necessary to ensure the accuracy of claims submitted to government.

Troklus: In reading an article on long-term care, I understand that one of the goals of PPS is to give incentives to providers to control utilization and costs. How do you feel that can best be accomplished without affecting quality of care?

Altman: You have touched on one of the most difficult aspects of compliance issues in long-term care. The government has claimed that, under the previous cost-based reimbursement system, overutilization and, therefore, overbilling were rampant. One goal of the prospective payment system was to reduce utilization. Now the government is concerned that, with the advent of a fixed-price prospective payment system, the incentive to contain costs could result in the inappropriate *underutilization* of services, which would compromise quality of care. Frankly, I think this policy per-

---

[1] Diagnosis Related Group

spective puts providers in somewhat of a vise, particularly with respect to some of the therapy services, which the government firmly believes were overutilized before PPS. Those services are no longer being provided in the same scope and amount, which is one of the government's primary goals. On the other hand, providers are put in the position of having to justify the discrepancy in the scope and volume of services provided pre- and post-PPS.

When I was in law school, my trial practice instructor always characterized it as the fantasy of any lawyer to catch a witness on the stand in a contradiction, so that with great drama he or she could ask the witness, "Were you lying then or are you lying now?" That is a situation long-term care providers find themselves in with respect to this issue of quality of care under prospective payment. To me, the only answer is that providers must provide a clinical justification for all decisions made with respect to care under the prospective payment system and make sure that the clinical documentation supports those decisions.

The prospective payment system was much more than a simple change in the reimbursement system. It was also a change by the policy makers in the clinical service delivery system. As just one example, prior to PPS, respiratory therapists, physical therapists, occupational therapists, and speech therapists who were reimbursed separately under a cost-based system were very involved in assessing and carrying out the care plans of individual residents. However, a natural consequence of going to a fixed-priced prospective system is that responsibility is, perhaps appropriately, vested in nursing staff to conduct a comprehensive assessment of residents and to organize and coordinate the provision of all of these services. Therefore, there is a clinical justification in many cases for providing a different scope and volume of these therapy services post-PPS if nursing is now driving the interdisciplinary care process. These kinds of clinical justifications, from a compliance perspective, are important when addressing the government's concerns.

Troklus: I read an article you wrote in the March/April 1999 *Journal of Health Care Compliance* regarding quality of care as a compliance issue in long-term care. Do you have any suggestions on how to include quality of care in the compliance program?

Altman: Again, this is one of the more challenging compliance issues faced by long-term care compliance officers. Many people are not yet willing to characterize quality as a compliance issue, even when the government clearly defines it as such. My advice for long-term care compliance officers is to understand the philosophy and orientation of their organization with respect to quality. Some organizations with well-developed clinical operations functions choose to vest primary responsibility for quality of care as a compliance issue in that existing clinical operations function. In that case, the role of the compliance officer is limited to coordinating the response to quality of care concerns raised by regulators. The compliance officer may simply ensure that the organization has policies, procedures, and systems in place to address compliance with quality of care requirements. On the other hand, an organization may provide the compliance function with the resources to independently ensure that quality of care is being delivered and that systems exist to identify quality problems before the regulators identify them for the organization. In this case, the role of the compliance officer is more direct with respect to quality. With the latter design, there is much more potential for conflict between the compliance function and the existing clinical operations function, and that conflict must always be mediated by the compliance officer.

In either case, we should be beyond the point of asking whether quality of care is a compliance issue. Instead, organizations need to determine how they are going to address quality of care as a compliance issue. It is incumbent upon the compliance officer to develop an organizational response that not only meets the regulators' concerns with respect to quality of care, but does so in a manner that reflects the philosophy and orientation of the company and of the clinicians who ultimately are responsible for delivering quality of care.

Non–long-term care health care providers should take careful note of the development of quality of care as a compliance issue. This trend is not limited to long-term care; the government will most likely characterize quality of care as a compliance issue for other sectors of the health care provider community. While many might view this prospect as a threat and inappropriate, I view it as an opportunity. Health care providers, given the public erosion of trust and highly publicized extent of medical errors, should use this trend as an opportunity to define for themselves how they want to treat quality of care as a compliance issue.

Troklus: Do you have a few tips for other long-term care facilities struggling with the implementation of a compliance program?

Altman: Many organizations, including provider organizations and compliance organizations, already have well-developed materials that providers can use so they can avoid re-creating the wheel. The Health Care Compliance Association, in particular, has been useful in developing some very practical materials and tips on implementing compliance programs. Also, we should increase collaboration between long-term care providers on fundamental compliance issues so that we can all save our limited resources. PPS is a perfect example of this. Organizations should not be on their own in figuring out approaches to complying with the ever-changing and complex requirements related to PPS. We should pool our resources and rely on each other's expertise to develop an industrywide response. And the government should support such collaborative efforts.

Troklus: What background experience and/or credentials do you feel are important for a compliance officer in a long-term care facility?

Altman: While I have found my legal training to be a great asset, I certainly do not think it is a prerequisite. Probably the most important attribute of an effective compliance officer in long-term care is knowledge of the industry, the challenges faced by the industry, and the unique attributes of the long-term care worker, particularly at the facility level. Compliance is a very difficult, but in many ways rewarding, sector of the health care community. Compliance officers will be most effective if they understand the unique nature of long-term care. Beyond that, the compliance officer could come from a clinical, billing, legal, or reimbursement background and perform effectively. Compliance officers must recognize their own limitations and seek participation and guidance from others in areas in which they do not have expertise. For example, if a clinical person is serving as a long-term care compliance officer, he or she must engage the assistance of individuals with reimbursement expertise in order to address those other compliance issues.

Troklus: What advice do you have for compliance officers attempting to conduct background checks?

Altman: This is a very difficult issue for long-term care compliance officers, particularly those in multi-facility organizations, because of the very high turnover rate in nursing home workers. One piece of advice I have is to regularly check the OIG's Sanction database, which is relatively easy to do through the Internet. In our organization, we developed a computer program that links the database with the payroll system so that we can automatically and regularly check any new hires with a minimum of effort. Of course, the development of that system required upfront work, but the long-term benefits have already paid off.

The issue of background checks is one in which I again would call for industrywide collaboration. The government has identified background checks as an important measure to protect the safety and welfare of residents, yet it has not provided any tangible support in the development of a national database on nurse aides or other health care workers. Only the federal government has the resources to create such a database, and therefore federal policy makers should devote resources to the creation of such a database. This is a perfect example of where public policy concerns and the interest of the providers coincide, yet there has not been enough constructive collaboration to address the issue that both have identified.

Troklus: What training approach works best for long-term care facilities?

Altman: Because of the high turnover rate of employees, training is a challenge for the long-term care compliance officer. On the other hand, effective training can, in fact, reduce turnover and improve the quality of care in long-term care facilities, which makes it vitally important. Different training approaches must be developed to accommodate the different levels and backgrounds of long-term care employees. Many of our long-term care workers have limited education, and some do not have English as a first language. Our training needs to reflect that reality and be delivered in a manner that can be effectively comprehended by our workers. In addition, certain aspects of the reimbursement system, particularly the new prospective payment system, are very complex and will require a different level of training for workers in that area. In this regard, the OIG's guidance does reflect the realities of long-term care operations in its recommendation that the organization provide both general compliance training and specific compliance training targeted to specific job responsibilities.

Troklus: Should training be mandatory or voluntary?

Altman: From the government's perspective, compliance programs are voluntary; so I suppose that training should also be voluntary. But from the provider's perspective, all employees should have training available to them and all employees should be required to attend that training. The challenge is to not allow training to be a mandatory requirement that people come to resent, but instead to foster the view that training is an opportunity to increase employee competence, professional growth, and loyalty to the company. And I would generalize that attitude to all aspects of the compliance program. The tendency is to view compliance as external to operations and as a necessary evil. The most effective thing that a long-term care compliance officer can do is to instill an environment in the company in which compliance becomes integrated with operations and viewed by all employees as an important part of the way the provider does business and delivers care. This point is especially important with respect to training.

Troklus: In the Health Insurance Portability and Accountability Act's [HIPAA] proposed privacy standards, someone must be designated the "privacy official." Should it be the compliance officer?

Altman: The answer to that question depends very much on the structure, philosophy, and orientation of the company. The compliance officer plays a critical role in developing a plan to implement the HIPAA requirements. In our organization, I, as the compliance officer, have been charged with coordinating a companywide strategic plan to meet the HIPAA requirements. Whether I will ultimately be designated as the privacy official is a decision that should be deferred until the company develops a strategic plan to meet HIPAA standards. I do think that it makes sense for the compliance officer to coordinate an organizational response to the HIPAA requirements.

Troklus: What do you see as effective reporting mechanisms?

Altman: Certainly one effective reporting mechanism is a compliance hotline. But if an employee has to resort to reporting a compliance issue through the compliance hotline, communication in the organization has broken down somewhere along the chain of command. Ideally, the most effective reporting mechanism is one in which every employee feels he or she can approach his or her supervisor or others in the chain of command and raise compliance issues without the fear of retribution and with the confidence that the issue will be addressed. There will always be situations in which employees do not feel that that avenue is appropriate, so the hotline is very important. But through training and the way the compliance program is implemented, the compliance officer should create an open environment in which employees do not fear retaliation in raising legitimate compliance concerns.

Troklus: What is your opinion regarding marketing of hotlines? Should the number be furnished to patients and/or displayed where patients can see?

Altman: Again, the answer to that question depends very much on the philosophy and orientation of the company. I can tell you how we addressed this issue. In addition to the compliance hotline, we market and provide to patients and families of patients a phone number that we call our "ASAP" line. This line is meant for patients and families who have concerns about their care or other aspects of their experience with our facilities and cannot get those issues addressed at the facility level. The ASAP line provides an additional avenue of communication for their concerns. In fact, the phone number of the ASAP line is the same as the compliance hotline number. We integrated the lines so we would have a centralized way to track, trend, and address these issues as they arise. As you might imagine, there is some overlap between the substance of issues that come in on the ASAP line and those that come in on the compliance hotline.

We felt it important that patients and family members have their own set of marketing materials to make sure they understood that there were alternative ways to get issues addressed. We also felt it important that employees have their own avenue for addressing issues.

Troklus: What advice do you have for someone who is considering compliance as a profession?

Altman: First, it is definitely a high-risk/high-reward career path. The position of compliance officer is a very difficult one, and it is easy to feel isolated and weighed down by the responsibility of ensuring compliance in such a heavily regulated, unpredictable, and aggressive enforcement environment. At the same time, ensuring that an organization complies with the complex web of regulations while meeting its primary mission of providing quality of care can be extremely rewarding. Second, anyone considering becoming a long-term care compliance officer should carefully evaluate the commitment of senior management of the long-term care provider to compliance. The position of long-term care compliance officer is fraught with risk in those organizations in which senior management is not committed to developing, implementing, and continually modifying its compliance program to meet the challenges facing all long-term care providers.

Interview 3

F. Lisa Murtha
KPMG

F. Lisa Murtha is chief audit and compliance officer for Childrens Hospital of Philadelphia. Ms. Murtha has extensive experience in health care law, compliance, and investigations experience.

Troklus: Let's talk about your tenure as a compliance officer.

Murtha: My first compliance program actually was developed in 1993 when I was working for a national rehabilitation hospital company. As you know, that was shortly after the passage of the Federal Sentencing Guidelines. Our company was a publicly traded organization, and our general counsel wanted to be very proactive about compliance. He felt that being a publicly traded organization, working in health care, and seeing what had recently happened to National Medical Enterprises, which was one of our competitors, we really needed to be on the front end of the compliance initiative. He assigned responsibility to me to help develop a compliance program for our organization and deliver it to all thirty-nine hospitals and nursing homes. That was my first foray into the whole realm of corporate compliance, and I have to say that even though I was a health care lawyer and worked in the health care industry for my whole career, I had never done anything like that. It is so interesting to take the law and regulations and try to incorporate them very actively into a working health care organization. As we all know, that is not necessarily an easy task.

Troklus: What got you interested in compliance?

Murtha: My first experience in the compliance field in 1993 was a way for me to be a positive part of helping to change culture in an organization. Again, coming to compliance from the legal perspective, you are often faced with dealing with all the problems and never really being part of the solution. What I loved about compliance was that for the first time in my career, I could really be part of the solution. Not only could I help turn an organization's risks into positive scenarios, I could be part of changing the ethical culture of the organization, which was quite gratifying personally.

Troklus: What was the most interesting part of your job as compliance officer?

Murtha: Actually, at that particular organization I was not designated as the compliance officer. Our senior vice president and chief financial officer actually became the compliance officer. I was just in a supporting role for him. My first compliance officer job came in 1995 with Pennsylvania Blue Shield. After our organization went through a large investigation with the federal government, our board decided that the company needed to develop and implement a compliance program. Because I had worked on a project like that before, the president and board asked me to take the compliance officer job. The most interesting part of that job was getting involved in training and education. I found that in the compliance arena, problems often occurred not because people intended for them to happen, but because they really didn't understand or appreciate what the laws and regulations required. With training and education, I saw such a vast improvement in people's knowledge levels, not only in terms of the laws and regulations, but also in how the laws and regulations applied to their particular jobs. They wanted to do the right thing; they just didn't have any guidance in the past. Again, it was very gratifying because they were thankful for the guidance they received.

Troklus: What challenges do you see a compliance officer facing on a day-to-day basis?

Murtha: As all of us know who have been in the compliance arena, there are many challenges. I think the biggest one that I experienced was resistance from management. Managers tend to keep you at arm's length because they fear that the closer you get, the greater the potential that you'll find problems in their areas. They certainly don't want problems to be exposed; and if they are exposed, the managers would rather be the ones to do so. One of the really positive ways you can approach them is to say, "Listen, even if problems are identified, that is not unusual. You cannot be all things to all people, and there are few organizations that comply with all laws and all regulations at every point in time." From the operational perspective, if you are part of the solution and implement the correction, you are a hero. People in management often accept that perspective gratefully. You can turn their fear around by letting them know that you are there as a very positive force to help support them to get the job done.

Troklus: Was the transition from compliance officer to compliance consultant difficult?

Murtha: No, I found that the transition was fairly easy, because in the compliance officer role, you really are a consultant. You are a consultant to management, and you are a consultant to the clinicians on what the laws and the regulations require and how clinicians might achieve compliance with those laws and regulations. For all intents and purposes, that is what I do now in the actual consulting arena. Clients come to us with every variation on how to implement a compliance program, including very technical issues, everything from life Medicare/Medicaid reimbursement to clinical concerns. The very best compliance officers are the ones that are viewed not necessarily as enforcers, but as consultants to management.

Troklus: Have organizations generally moved past the implementation stage to questions of effectiveness?

Murtha: Absolutely. Surprisingly enough, there are still many organizations out there that do not have anything in the way of a compliance program or compliance infrastructure, which is quite surprising given what we see in the newspapers practically every day. Having said that, we are getting a lot of requests to come in and review the effectiveness of compliance programs or various aspects of compliance programs. It may be to review the coding and billing piece, cost reports, or the charge master. I find that everybody seems to be moving to what I would call a new generation of compliance, which is effectiveness. New areas such as research compliance are now being examined.

Troklus: Let's talk about education. Do you feel compliance training should be mandatory or voluntary?

Murtha: I think mandatory because, again, health care is one of the most complex, highly regulated industries in the world. It is impossible for people to have a full appreciation of their responsibilities unless they really understand what those laws and regulations require. I think training should be mandatory, but it doesn't have to be boring. The more interactive training is, the more fun it will be and the more people will ultimately get out of it.

Troklus: How many hours of training should be provided each year, and who should receive training?

Murtha: In terms of how many hours, obviously the Office of Inspector General recommends a minimum of one hour per year. I have found that one hour really is not enough. Even for general compliance training, in the organizations where I was the compliance officer, we found that two hours were needed in the first year, in large part because there were so many questions that grew out of the instruction. We needed to allow the appropriate amount of time to address those questions, because people want to understand what the laws and regulations mean in terms of what they do every day. Having said that, I think the sessions tend to last two hours even if you only schedule an hour.

In terms of the second part of your question, every single person in the institution should have some level of general compliance training. We all know that health care is an interesting industry, because you deal with people who may have no education beyond high school up to people who are some of the most highly educated in the world: physicians, researchers, investigators, etc. Even general compliance training needs to be geared toward the audience involved. But everybody across the board needs to have some level of training as it relates to their particular work areas.

Troklus: What are a few major focus areas that you feel compliance training should cover?

Murtha: The most effective compliance training that I have seen has covered general issues, everything from conflicts of interest to the acceptance and the giving of gifts and gratuities. That should be obviously very pertinent because many of the laws and regulations that deal with health care fraud and abuse touch on those issues, such as the anti-kickback statute and the Stark laws. I think that those are critical areas. General compliance training also should focus on creating and maintaining an ethical workplace, and what that really means in health care. Compliance should be connected to the institution's social mission; for example, if the institution is Catholic or some other religious affiliation, the compliance initiative should be geared into the spiritual, ethical, and moral responsibilities of the institution. That is a very effective way to get the word out, and an approach that people seem to accommodate well.

Another critical focus area is dealing with institutional assets appropriately, making sure they are used for the intended purposes. Specialized training is really, really important and becoming even more important as the government grows more knowledgeable about health care and the nuances of reimbursement. Likewise, the employees who deal with those issues every day—those in the medical records department, those in the billing area, the individuals who develop the cost reports, and those involved in research—need to be intimately involved and aware of those laws and regulations and how they may change from year to year. Creating some sort of system and educating employees on how to use the Internet to look at changes that the Office of Inspector General may issue or that intermediaries or carriers may issue is critical. In some special training areas we are seeing a lot of activity with cost reporting, charge master work, coding (which is always going to be a key area), and ambulatory payment classifications. Most recently, our firm has received more requests related to the HIPAA[1] privacy provision. Even though the proposed rule for HIPAA has not been finalized, we have some idea of where the government is heading, and we know that there are many items in the proposed rule that will remain in the final rule. Health care organizations are now trying to understand how they can get up to speed when the rule is finally posted.

---

[1] Health Insurance Portability and Accountability Act

Troklus: In HIPAA, I have seen the comment that there should be a privacy officer. Do you see the compliance officer having to fill that role?

Murtha: That seems to be the feeling from most of the hospital organizations that I have been dealing with lately. They seem to think it is a natural fit. One could argue that many compliance officers, although they may have tremendous legal, finance, or operational backgrounds, don't possess one critical skill set that is going to be required on an ongoing basis with HIPAA. They do not have expertise with technology's role in privacy issues as the institution and the health care industry become more technology-driven. If compliance officers ultimately assume the role of privacy officers, they will either need to be educated on those issues, or they are going to need to forge a very strong alliance with the technology staffs in their organizations. So far, it does seem to be the compliance officer taking on responsibility for HIPAA.

Troklus: Do you feel it is better to conduct training in-house or to use external resources?

Murtha: I really believe in using internal resources because compliance issues come up all the time, and you need to have ready access to people and resources that can give you the answers you need. That can help you avoid major issues down the road. Further, the more that compliance training can be done internally, the more people will be accountable for compliance. If they have to educate themselves enough to train others in the department, for example, then not only are they going to know more, but they are going to take ownership in the ultimate outcomes. Ownership and accountability are absolutely critical, because even a compliance officer—as good as he or she may be—cannot be entirely responsible for compliance with every law and regulation. It has got to be everyone's responsibility.

Troklus: What do you see as the major training challenges for compliance officers?

Murtha: There are a number of challenges. The first challenge is figuring out how to get all those people trained within a reasonable time frame. One widespread approach is cascading training, in which you start at the top of the organization and work your way down through management. Once you get to the level of the department heads, you may provide them with sessions that give answers to commonly asked questions that are likely to be facing them from time to time. Then the department directors actually do the balance of the training for the people in their departments, a "train-the-trainers" approach. A second challenge is finding more interesting ways to train staff. For example, as opposed to straight lectures, we can use case studies, videos, Internet training, or some other technology format. The more interactive the training is, the more people tend to like it. Trying to understand the best approach for your organization is always an issue. Of course, financing the training is often a concern. Although you may have a lot of creative ideas about how to train your employees, you may not have the financial resources to implement those ideas. The good news is that as time goes on, more and more organizations and more and more vendors are developing "off-the-shelf" training products. It may not be the entire answer, but it can at least spice up a lecture. Never underestimate the power of a visual approach. Making sure that the training money is used effectively can be a challenge as well.

Troklus: Educating physicians can be a challenge. What methods of training do you suggest work best for physicians?

Murtha: Physicians are probably the toughest group to train, for so many reasons, not the least of which is simply their lack of time. I like to separate the physicians by specialty or by department, as the case may be. One effective method is to give them an overview of what the fraud and abuse environment really is and how it relates to them. I talk to them about some of the laws and regulations that effect them on a day to day basis, from the anti-kickback statute, to how the government uses the False Claims Act to investigate and prosecute fraud and abuse, to specific cases in which physicians have been found to violate the fraud and abuse laws and what the ramifications were. I discuss issues on a department-by-department basis, such as obtaining a sample of medical records in their departments and performing a documentation and coding review to determine where that particular department is with compliance. Presenting that information with overhead transparencies is a good way to illustrate to the doctors examples of great documentation that supports the coding that was ultimately billed. Likewise, I can identify where the documentation fell short and what should have been done to correct it. The doctors can not say, "That's all well and good, but we would never do that in our department." It is specific to their specialty, which I think is critical, because the coding is driven by the diagnosis, the specialty, and what the doctor specifically does to the patient. I would also mention that the ultimate training is training available in a technology format that would be available at convenient times and places for the doctors. That is certainly nirvana from the training perspective with doctors, because again, one of the biggest challenges is actually getting them in a room and making them sit there without their beepers or cell phones interrupting.

Troklus: What do you think about pre- and posttests for educational purposes?

Murtha: They can be very effective in a lot of ways. They can really focus people on what they think they know and what they do not know. In the clinical arena, the physicians can feel like they know it all. They do not really think that they need to waste their time with the type of training and education that is typically involved with compliance. A pre- and posttest can really illustrate for them that all of us can benefit from some appropriate training and education in these areas. In the long run, there is an inherent benefit and the time is well spent. Therefore, I believe the tests can be very effective. So far though, I have not seen them widely utilized because there is an issue related to people being offended by having to be tested in some of these areas. Once you can get them over that, the tests can be quite effective.

Troklus: How can a compliance officer measure education and training effectiveness?

Murtha: When the rubber meets the road, it's actually "how compliant are you after the fact?" Effectiveness is most often measured using compliance monitoring activities. In the physician arena, it may be performing a prediagnostic review of documentation and coding in and among the various departments, having everyone trained, and then going back three months later to see if the error rate has decreased. That can be very illustrative of what people have learned and where potential issues may still remain. When it comes to other areas, there may be a diagnostic review on the front end identifying the potential issues. Focus training on the areas where risks were identified, and then go back in three to six months to make sure that compliance has improved, again utilizing your monitoring capabilities/resources. This really tells you a lot in terms of whether the training was effective, whether people benefited from it in the long run, and whether it really did its job at decreasing the risks.

Troklus: What are three key pieces of information that every employee needs to know regarding compliance?

Murtha: Number one, compliance is everyone's responsibility. Two, we all have a duty to report noncompliance on an ongoing basis. It is a very flowing sort of process, one without a beginning and an end. It is a part of everything we do every single day. Third, people need to know and feel comfortable that there will be no retribution for coming forward to report issues on an ongoing basis. If they get to that point, then they are likely to feel comfortable questioning various activities; they may not know what the law is in a particular area, but they may have a gut feeling that what is being done is not correct. If they know they have the duty to come forward, that it is their responsibility, then they are likely to do the right thing: come forward, get the questions answered, and fix what needs to be fixed.

Troklus: Do you have any advice for obtaining buy-in and commitment from physicians?

Murtha: That is always difficult. Number one, it helps to give them some preliminary information by way of short lectures or taking five to ten minutes at departmental meetings to explain to them what the compliance program is and how it will benefit them. In fact, not only will they benefit from having more information and better information about how to do their jobs correctly, certainly from the reimbursement perspective, doctors will also learn that compliance is not just about adding more responsibility; in the end, they benefit financially as well. We have been able to track, at least for our clients, that once compliance training with physicians is performed, reimbursement actually goes up. People learn that there are areas where they could have been billing and they never did because they did not know any better. In other areas, because the documentation is more complete, they can justify higher levels in coding, levels that better reflect the work that was actually done with the patient. Once physicians keep an open mind, then they are believers and they will absolutely cooperate. My sense is that unless you actually demonstrate the positive benefits to them—that their reimbursement goes up or that they have less risk with the government—you are never going to make them true believers.

Troklus: Many physicians don't like the idea of having a sanction check run on them. Do you feel that sanction checks are necessary?

Murtha: I do. I really do. The bottom line is that typical credentialing, although it can be very good and very effective, may not pick up a lot of these things. Ongoing sanction checks are important to any institution to demonstrate the institution's commitment to compliance and to making sure that everything is on the "up and up." It is also important to acknowledge that there are problem areas that can be dealt with effectively. That does not necessarily mean that the physicians are in trouble or need to leave the organization, just that there is some sort of explanation provided for why there may be a problem, that it has been documented, and that everybody is on board. For example, if physicians are suspended from providing services under CHAMPUS, they will be debarred under all government programs. Having said that, they may or may not be in a position to do work. As long as the institution knows that, it can take the appropriate action to limit liability.

Troklus: Who do you feel should be included in sanction checks?

Murtha: That is absolutely the toughest issue that people are dealing with right now. It is really a cost and resource issue. Certainly all physicians should be checked, as well as clinicians who require licensure or who deal in direct patient care, individuals who deal with reimbursement or the organization's money, and anyone who deals with or has access to pharmaceuticals. Those seem to be the highest risk areas in the organization, and if possible, it would be great if those categories of employees could be checked. But again, sometimes it is a resource issue and a cost issue. The more that the compliance infrastructure in the organization can accommodate checks internally, the better. They can use the Internet or other search tools that are available on the open market today. They can also deal directly with the local police department, etc.

Troklus: What challenges can a new compliance officer expect when going through the implementation phase of the compliance program?

Murtha: The first challenge is one of expectations and timing. Often new compliance officers take on this responsibility with that certain "joie de vivre," with the attitude that they will make this a better place for all of us to live. That is great, and that type of enthusiasm is really to be applauded. However, I don't think people should have unrealistic expectations about what can be done and within what time frame. Culture change takes time. It took years and years to develop that organizational culture; it will take a lot of time to change it. Even simple little nuances sometimes take a long time. You have got to be very patient and understand that people have to rethink the way they do things. That is somewhat traumatic for some people and creates a lot of anxiety in an organization. Be patient and understanding and know that the implementation is going to take some time.

Troklus: Do things get any easier over time?

Murtha: It is a hard question to answer. I think things do get easier from the perspective that people at least have a familiarity with what a compliance program is, what it means to the organization, and how they are supposed to deal with it. However, there are always going to be issues. The organization is never going to be perfect. If you go into it thinking that you are going to fix everything that needs to be fixed, you will be left feeling somewhat let down. That is not easy, and I think that may be why some compliance officers get a little disheartened after awhile. They feel like they have put their body, mind, and soul into the program and they are not seeing the reaction to compliance issues that they would like to see. But again, you need to be patient, because culture change takes time. Even though the changes will accrue over time, it is a slow process.

Troklus: Where do you see compliance in the next five years?

Murtha: Compliance is going to become a very integral part of the senior management of an organization. The Office of Inspector General recommends that compliance be situated at a high level, and it seems most organizations developing these programs are incorporating this recommendation into their own corporate infrastructures.

I also see compliance becoming more prominent in the news. Research compliance is one of the primary areas that is really hot right now—issues surrounding clinical trials and other aspects of research, as well as institutional review boards.

Regarding other areas of compliance, the nuances of facility designations may receive attention, such as whether an institution is appropriately designated as a long-term acute-care facility or whether it should be designated as a rehabilitation hospital. The question of whether the hospital's protocols support the designation that they have under Medicare or Medicaid is a compliance issue. Some of these more technical areas are going to be the wave of the future.

Last, we are going to see how technology can help an organization be more compliant. Technology answers many challenges that we are facing today, whether it's training, ways to monitor, or how to utilize the institutions' existing software and hardware to perform compliance checks.

Troklus: What advice would you have for a new compliance officer?

Murtha: The best advice I could give new compliance officers is to let them know that although their job will be challenging on a day-to-day basis, it can be one of the most gratifying experiences of their career. The more they can initially appreciate the culture of the organization and understand who the players are, the more effective they can be in the long term. Initially, they really need to get the lay of the land and to do their homework before they attempt to start making changes. Sometimes it's not so much what you say, but how you say it that means the difference between success and failure.

Interview 4

Joe Beck
Quorum Health Resources, LLC

Mr. Beck coordinates the compliance efforts for Quorum Healthcare's managed hospitals. Working with over 200 hospitals is challanging enough, but there is added complexity when those hospitals are managed and not owned. Many of us deal with organizations that we do not own and Mr. Beck's experience, ideas, and strategies for implementing compliance program is invaluable.

Snell: Describe your organization for us.

Beck: Quorum Health Resources manages over 200 hospitals and also provides consulting services to hospitals nationwide. The company is eleven years old and is in forty-three states.

Snell: How long have you been in the health care business?

Beck: My most recent stint with health care has been about twelve years. After college, I was with a hospital in New Orleans for about six years. I then left the health care industry and went into the energy industry. I came back into health care and was with Charter Medical before coming to Quorum.

Snell: The energy industry, that is interesting. Some of the companies in the energy industry are starting to implement compliance programs. Had you run into that at all when you were in the energy industry?

Beck: We found very often in that industry that compliance was just something that we did because the energy industry was highly regulated; it was the nature of business. A "compliance program" was not a prevalent term within the context that we mention it now in the health care industry. Looking back, I feel health care today is more regulated than the energy industry when I was there.

Snell: How does your organization distribute responsibility for compliance-related activities?

Beck: I work closely with Quorum's 200 managed hospitals. Typically, CEOs and CFOs are Quorum employees who report to the board, and we work with them in supporting and following the directions of the local board of directors. Quorum Health Resources is organized into four divisions, which are broken down into a total of about twenty groups. Each group vice president works with six to ten hospitals. We all communicate regularly through e-mail, and have periodic group and division meetings.

Snell: Of all the compliance activities you have been engaged in, which one did you personally find the most interesting?

Beck: There have been so many, it is hard to say. With 200 hospitals there are many interesting perspectives. One place where many of the perspectives come to light is our Compliance Officer Forum, an interactive program where we educate hospital compliance officers. In the last two years, we have probably educated some 500 people through that program. It is two days long, and it gives us the opportunity to meet not only compliance officers, but in many instances, board members, chief executive officers, and sometimes even local legal counsel. To watch their eyes light up once they begin to see and understand what the word "compliance" really means has been a very interesting personal experience for me. For many, you can see that they understand that it is not the end of the world as they know it but a world with many new rules. It is something they do need to understand to be able to integrate compliance into their daily operations.

Snell: Where have you received the best compliance-related ideas or information?

Beck: I would have to say that the Internet is a fabulous resource for so many things today. I belong to various listservs and search the Internet periodically. Also, I visit the Office of Inspector General web site, and I belong to a couple of its listservs. There is nothing like going to the source of the data. I also visit the American Hospital Association's web site and the Health Care Compliance Association's web site—to name a couple.

There are certainly some individuals with whom I have had an opportunity to work with over the years who have been very insightful and very systems oriented. I believe they were very important, not only for me, but also for our organization to be affiliated with. It's very important, for something as complex and broad in scope as compliance, that a systematic approach be used and everything be broken down into as small and concise elements as possible.

Snell: Can you give me an example of systems thinking or systematizing a piece of compliance?

Beck: Checklists, lots of checklists. One that immediately comes to mind is an implementation checklist. It is a tool for compliance officers that provides a comprehensive list of everything imaginable that is health care compliance related. Compliance officers use the checklist to determine what is applicable to their institution and what is not. For example, Federal Aviation Administration regulations require hospitals to train employees who package and air ship biohazardous materials to labs, etc. Such regulations may not be applicable to every hospital. By using the checklist, compliance officers can determine what regulations they need to comply with and develop action plans to do so.

Snell: What actions have you taken to get your board or boards involved in compliance?

Beck: About two years before the OIG issued its guidance on compliance for hospitals, we provided tools and education on compliance and business ethics to our managed hospitals, and group vice presidents began educating boards about compliance. Additionally, our Foundations for the Future Programs educate trustees on a variety of responsibilities of their role, including compliance and business ethics.

Snell: What type of background for an individual trustee has been most helpful when you have gone to meet with boards?

Beck: Hospital board members come from very broad and diverse backgrounds. Most of them are business people from their communities. The thing they really have in common is that they all care about their hospitals and their communities.

There are some trustees who really do take to the subject of compliance. They are often people who were involved in compliance or regulatory concerns in another industry, and it is natural for them to have that interest as well in their role as trustee.

Snell: You said you work mostly with the hospitals that you manage. Do you see a difference between the way you have to deal with managed hospitals versus owned hospitals on compliance programs?

Beck: Yes. Philosophically, our perspective is that we assist managed hospitals in the implementation of their programs. We work with them by providing tools, educational and templates that they customize and build into the fabric of their organization. The scope is very broad. I typically don't get involved in the day-to-day operational issues related to their compliance concerns. If the hospital is owned, a great deal of time is spent day in and day out on problem solving and reengineering of the hospital and the department functions.

Snell: Are there any standardized policies or procedures in Quorum-managed hospitals?

Beck: No, the templates we provide hospitals are standardized, but every hospital customizes the templates to reflect its operations and services. There are also local and state regulations hospitals must consider in their policies and procedures, so each template has to be customized. What we have learned with 200 hospitals is that they might supply similar kinds of services, but no two of them are alike.

Snell: Do the hospitals distribute their code of conduct to all of their employees? Do you have any recommendations?

Beck: Absolutely! The code of conduct is a way for an organization to communicate its values and mission to its employees. A hospital can create all the policies and procedures it wants and at some point an employee is going to deal with an issue that is not covered by policy or procedure. It is very important for employees to understand the organization's ethics and values so that they have ethical guideposts to provide direction when they deal with an issue that isn't prescribed by policy.

Snell: What is one of the most significant accomplishments that you have had with regard to compliance?

Beck: Based on recent information, it appears that a large number of organizations with which we work are very involved in reengineering various processes in many different departments. Reengineering at the department level is truly the essence of compliance. Through reengineering, compliance becomes embedded in the organization; it simply becomes the way they operate. Reengineering is how you build it in, not just add it on. It has been very encouraging to see hospitals get to a point where they are really wrestling with building in compliance, they are beyond the basics of hotlines and background checks. Maybe for a noncompliance person that may not be thrilling, but I can tell you, for me, it is thrilling to see organizations really moving down the continuum and getting things done.

Snell: What is one of the most difficult compliance tasks today?

Beck: Clearly, I think one of the most difficult tasks is keeping the momentum going. It seems organizations in health care today have to do more and more in a shorter period of time, and with dwindling resources. It is incredible to see them juggle the priorities that are necessary to maintain progress in compliance, and then have to shift gears and work on Y2K, then shift back to compliance, then shift to get ready for APCs, then shift back to compliance; and they will soon have to shift again to get ready for HIPAA. You take all of these changes and it is just absolutely miraculous that the organizations are able to do what they are doing. There is a piece of me that says, "My God, the industry is doing all these things and our primary mission is not to do this, but to take care of sick people." It is incredible that organizations that are professional health care providers have also had to become overnight experts in business information technology, millions of pages of laws and related regulations at the federal, state, and local levels, and have their revenues slashed, and still be expected to provide the highest level of quality care in the world. It is just remarkable.

Snell: I keep thinking about what type of people really understand this stuff called compliance. There are many similar fields that we can bring qualified people forward into compliance. We have the legal, risk management, quality improvement, and quality assurance professionals. Has anything been done in related fields or departments that relates closely to the compliance effort?

Beck: I believe creating a compliance culture and maintaining it is really a continuous quality improvement (CQI) endeavor. It is something that never ends. It is something that organizations are going to do forever, and they will continue to reengineer and reinvent themselves as the laws and regulations change, and we know that never ends. Health care organizations have already been doing this from a "JCAHO"[1] perspective for years. I think people who have a CQI perspective, an orientation to develop and use the systems, and who have good education and communica-

---

[1] Joint Commission on Accreditation of Healthcare Organizations

tion skills are probably some of the best folks to be able to drive compliance initiatives.

Snell: What about an anonymous reporting mechanism? Have you been able to help standardize that?

Beck: We have worked with organizations to help them understand the importance of having an anonymous reporting mechanism. I think a frustrating situation for some is "when that phone doesn't ring." We try to help them understand that it may not necessarily be a bad thing. Ideally, if their program is working well, employees will freely engage their supervision or compliance officer to address any concerns they may have. An anonymous reporting mechanism becomes a safety net in the event employees feel they can't use the chain of command. A reporting mechanism is like homeowner's insurance—it's something you hope you don't need, but you shouldn't cancel it because you don't use it. Some organizations will, depending on their economic resources, try to find the least costly way to set up a reporting mechanism. But we have found that an anonymous reporting mechanism that enables callers to have a means to call back and check on the status of their concern gives you a lifeline to them. If callers use this "call-back feature," you can either ask them more questions or communicate that you heard them and you are trying to move forward in reviewing their concern. Having some means to stay in touch with callers is a very important part of any reporting mechanism.

Snell: Do you actually give them a code number or any way to call back in? Have you heard of any techniques like that?

Beck: We work with a strategic service partner, the Pinkerton Service Group, who provides hotline intake services. They provide callers a call-back identification number that enables them to contact Pinkerton with a designated time frame to determine the status of their concern.

Snell: Have you ever measured the effectiveness of a compliance program in one of the hospitals or a component of it?

Beck: We have looked at some components and at this time are engaged in the development of additional assessments and audit process pilots.

Snell: What areas do you think the enforcement communities are focusing on now?

Beck: There seem to be so many. It depends on the local U.S. attorney's office and their current hot button. We continue to hear about activities related to lab unbundling and coding. We have heard about raids of armed agents on facilities that sometimes sound unbelievable, but they have been thoroughly documented and appear to be true.

Snell: What do you mean raids?

Beck: For example, I am aware of a nonaffiliated community hospital that was raided by government agents wearing flack jackets and pistols. They stated they were responding to an anonymous call of alleged billing fraud in their home health care agency and felt force was necessary to secure related documentation. We have heard of similar occurrences in other communities.

I have opportunities to do some public speaking and sometimes mention the particulars of such raids. Often, after the presentation, folks will come up and relate similar occurrences in their communities. It's remarkable that the media hasn't jumped on what appears to be a national story that armed agents are busting into health care facilities, frightening both patients and employees.

Snell: Many health care organizations are losing money. Some have filed have chapter 11, and it's not just traditional hospitals but nursing homes, managed care hospitals, and physician group practices that are in financial dire straights. Are you aware of many organizations that are having financial trouble, and do you think this is a significant issue?

Beck: I do believe that it is a significant issue. Quorum Health Resources is often contacted by hospitals that are interested in establishing a business relationship with us. As part of our due diligence processes, we meet with trustees and hospital managers to determine how we can assist them. We find, in some instances, organizations are struggling to the point where it is difficult even for them to pay for the help they need. Circumstances are that difficult for many hospitals out there. It is hard to believe the American public really understands what is actually happening to the health care system from a financial perspective, and how that can affect patient care in the long run.

Snell: When the American public figures out what collectively society is doing to health care from a financial perspective, do you think it could take a while to reverse the things that have caused the financial stress?

Beck: We are a consumer society; if we can buy what we want, we are happy. It seems we can't anticipate that some things will no longer be available, and we are unhappy when we can't get what we want, when we want it. I think that the consumer is not any different when it comes to health care services. Consumers consider health care as they would any other kind of service. They believe they get it if they want or need it. I don't believe that consumers are really aware of the effects of financial cuts, fines, penalties, and the cost of settlement agreements on health care. It may be that the consumers won't understand until they can't find the service they want or need anywhere in their community. They then will start to ask why. At that point, it may be too late and the services may never be able to be reestablished in the consumers' community.

Snell: Do you think some of the financial woes are related to the enforcement activities or implementation of compliance programs?

Beck: Based upon what I read and what I have seen, creating voluntary compliance programs is not inexpensive. They take time and resources that are being diverted from other things like equipment and staff. Organizations operating under OIG corporate integrity agreements have huge expenses not related to reimbursing Medicare, but for fines, penalties, and following government mandates of the settlement agreements. I was reading a news article the other day about a hospital in the northeast that was fined a quarter of a million dollars for damages to the Medicare program, but they also had a five-year integrity agreement that was going to cost them a million dollars a year to meet government mandates. So, are their dollars being spent to deal with regulatory issues rather than delivering health care? It certainly seems so.

Snell: What quality or background does a compliance officer need to make that job work?

Beck: Good old-fashioned evangelical zeal! The compliance officer has a difficult row to hoe. It takes intelligence and persuasive communications skills to be really effective.

Snell: How long do you think compliance will be a major emphasis for enforcement in the health care community?

Beck: The government has moved regulatory compliance from industry to industry over the years. It has used compliance as a means of levying fines and it has become a self-perpetuating engine. The health care industry is heavily regulated. Some of the regulations are unclear. Some of the regulations are contradictory. There are untold volumes of regulations, and they are constantly changing. Some government agencies don't communicate very effectively with others. While that may not convey a pretty picture, the industry is making progress dealing with the regulatory environment. I believe as we make sufficient progress the emphasis will gradually ease. You asked, "How long?" I'd say some time after the next regulatory milestone, HIPAA–Administrative Simplification, is behind us.

Interview 5

Sue Prophet
American Health Information Management Association

Ms. Prophet is one of the most knowlegeable coding experts in the country. She is currently the coding director for the American Healthcare Information Management Association. Ms. Prophet shares her experiences with the reader and relates her knowledge to compliance issues we all face. As we all know, the center of our most significant challenges lies in coding and billing issues.

Snell: Tell the reader a little bit about your background.

Prophet: My educational background is a bachelor's degree in health information management. After college, I took our association's registry exam to become a registered record administrator, now known as a registered health information administrator. A number of years later, I pursued one of our newer credentials related to coding certification: the CCS or certified coding specialist. My working background is mainly in a hospital setting, originally as a coding supervisor over both inpatient and outpatient coding, then in data quality management, doing a lot of coding reviews and checking coding, and ultimately as a hospital utilization review director. From that position, I went to work for the American Health Information Management Association (AHIMA) where I oversee coding policy issues from a national perspective, representing the members' issues on both coding and compliance issues, developing educational products, writing articles, reviewing regulations, providing input to government agencies, and interacting with other associations. We try to make sure our members' interests are represented and that we are providing education both to our members and to others on coding and related issues, such as compliance.

Snell: What work has AHIMA done in the area of health care compliance?

Prophet: We provide education through seminars and workshops as well as a number of articles, both in our journal and in other publications related to compliance. We have developed some canned programs that people can take on the road to provide education on coding and compliance. We also have a number of coding workbooks that schools and workshops can use. We have provided input to all of the OIG[1] compliance program guidance documents. We developed, and just recently revised, our standards of ethical coding. We are one of the four cooperating parties responsible for developing standardized, consistent, clear, ICD-9-CM coding guidelines so that everyone is on the same wavelength and understands how to code accurately. We have also developed a Payer's Guide to Healthcare Data Quality and Integrity as an effort to educate the payers on why coding is so important—beyond just their individual payment policies and getting the claims paid—and to emphasize the importance of national data quality and integrity and conformity in coding rules.

Snell: In doing all that, you have met a lot of people, talked with a lot of people on the phone, and heard their frustrations that relate to compliance problems, particularly getting the organization to do the right thing. What kind of frustrations are you hearing from the folks that you help?

Prophet: Probably the biggest frustration is that a lot of organizations are developing "go around" compliance programs, which means they go around the physicians. The staff is supposed to work around the physicians, not bother them too much, not hassle them for more accurate documentation. The billing staff, coding staff, and ancillary department staff all work together to decrease billing and claims errors, but there is no real organizational commitment to correcting the underlying process problems, especially the fundamental problem that the documentation is so poor that no one can code accurately from it. The whole compliance arena would have been a great opportunity for the industry to say, "Hey, we have been putting up with this bad documentation for a long time. Now that we have the government behind us, let's nip it in the bud and do something about

---

[1] Office of Inspector General

it." Instead, I have seen a lot of really creative ways to get around the problem of poor documentation.

Snell: What advice would you give an organization that is creating these frustrations?

Prophet: The compliance committee needs to educate the administration of the organization and the board of directors about the whole compliance process and about the whole billing process. You cannot achieve compliance just from the facility staff perspective, with no physician commitment. Compliance cannot be achieved without addressing documentation issues. Your compliance program must include a review of the documentation and steps to be taken to improve the medical record documentation in order to support the coding. There is a lot of misunderstanding about what coding is. People think, if we just get all our coders certified and send them to all these workshops, and make sure their *Coding Clinic for ICD-9-CM* subscriptions are up to date, and educate them until they are saturated with coding knowledge, then somehow all of our problems will be solved and our claims will be the best in the country. Those efforts do address problems in coding itself, but most of the coding problems, especially in orga-

nizations that have good, well-trained coding staff, relate more to the quality of the underlying documentation than to the accuracy of the coding.

Snell: Given the complexities of the health care industry, is it possible to have simple rules and regulations?

Prophet: It probably is, but it is going to take a lot more than fine-tuning or even reengineering. We need to completely throw out what we have and start over. We are probably not in the near future, or even in the long term, going to achieve a single-payer type of system. We will probably rely on a patchwork of insurance companies and Medicare for a long time to come. But the problems and the complexities stem much more from the various regulations within a particular payer. If, instead of just adding layer upon layer of regulations to Medicare, we just threw out all the regulations and started over, it would be a much, much simpler world.

Snell: I know you're in communication with many professional coders from around the country. What is their biggest frustration?

Prophet: Probably conflicts between the payer's rules and the coding system rules and guidelines. On the one hand, the OIG compliance program guidances and even HCFA[2] say that you must follow the official ICD-9-CM coding guidelines promulgated by the American Hospital Association, American Health Information Management Association, Health Care Financing Administration, and National Center for Health Statistics and you must follow what the AMA[3] says for CPT. But sometimes payers, and even Medicare fiscal intermediaries and carriers, insist that you do something for a particular payment policy that directly conflicts with those coding rules and guidelines, which causes a great deal of angst for the coder. The second biggest frustration is probably the pressure to get more and more records processed and coded, with an ultimate compromise on coding quality. Coders may be asked to code without all of the documentation present in the record, and then the coder is blamed when all the codes aren't there.

---

[2]Health Care Financing Administration
[3]American Medical Association

Snell: What can an organization do to minimize these frustrations for its coders?

Prophet: The organization needs to support the coders more. They should work with the coders to educate payers about the problems, and even produce examples of how the current system is hurting the payers in the long run. As the payers start looking at data, utilization patterns, and resource patterns, they will see that the data are all over the place because their priority up until now has been getting individual claims processed, instead of looking at the long-term, greater value of coded data from an aggregate perspective.

Snell: What are some of the weaknesses coders have?

Prophet: There is a lack of formal coding training. Sometimes people are, in essence, taken off the street and handed a code book. They lack any solid foundation in anatomy, physiology, and medical terminology. Also, they are not all keeping up to date on the changing rules and guidelines; for example, they do not have current subscriptions to *CPT Assistant* or *Coding Clinic for ICD-9-CM*. And they do not read Medicare bulletins, so they don't really know what the current rules are.

Snell: What can they do to improve those weaknesses?

Prophet: They should definitely attend coding classes if they haven't had formal coding training. Find a mentor, perhaps in coding, who can help monitor their coding, review it, tell them where their weaknesses are, and direct them to resources to address some of those weaknesses. They should attend as much continuing education as they possibly can. Finally, they should make sure that their subscriptions to coding resources, such as *Coding Clinic* and *CPT Assistant*, are up to date and that they are getting the Medicare bulletins and the other resources that they need to keep abreast of new information.

Snell: Does AHIMA certify coders? What kind of classifications do you have?

Prophet: Yes, we do certify coders, and we have two classifications. One is for hospital-based coders and addresses both inpatient coding and hospital outpatient coding, which would cover both ICD-9 and CPT. Then we have a physician-based coding credential, which is for those coders working in a physician's office or group practice setting. Again, it would cover ICD-9 and CPT. The difference between the two is that the physician-based credential includes E&M coding and focuses on the type of coding performed in physicians' offices.

Snell: What does certification mean to the coders and their institutions?

Prophet: It demonstrates that the individual has mastered a certain set of essential skills for successful coding, which in today's compliance environment is an asset for an employer. He can be assured that the person had a certain baseline skill level. It provides recognition of the individual's coding skills. It could mean more self-confidence for the coders as far as what skills they do have, more respect, higher job satisfaction, in some cases a raise or promotion, and certainly increased marketability of their skills.

Snell: What does it take to get certified?

Prophet: Other than a high school diploma, there is no hard and fast prerequisite for writing the certification exam. However, the exams for both credentials are designed for mastery level; they are not designed for entry level. Statistics have shown that people do much better on the exam if they have three or more years of relevant coding experience, which means hospital experience for the hospital-based exam and physician's office experience for the physician's office exam.

Snell: In my opinion, five years ago coders were seen as clerical help. Has that changed?

Prophet: Yes, it started changing after DRGs[4] came in. Although there is still a lack of awareness of coding as a profession, people outside the field are slowly beginning to realize what is involved in coding, how complex it is, and the type of knowledge necessary to be a successful coder. We get a lot of calls from U.S. attorney's offices and attorney general's offices, for

---

[4]Diagnostic Related Groups

example, that want someone to just run over to their office and give them an hour of coding training. They believe that small investment will enable them to do their investigations and their chart reviews and can make them expert coders. My answer to that is, "Would you like to have an R.N. taking care of you who received an hour of nursing training?" I tell them we have one- and two-year programs in coding and that years of experience are required before you can consider yourself an expert coder. A lot of people outside the coding profession still have no idea what it really takes.

Snell: Some people feel that it is hard to find good professional coders. What is your perception of the supply and demand in this area?

Prophet: The demand is much greater than the supply right now. The new emphasis on compliance and correct coding increases the demand for qualified coders, as has the implementation of the APC system, which also depends heavily on coding. Right now, more organizations are looking for coders than there are coders. There are stories of coders being called on the job by recruiters and other organizations that try to lure them away with attractive features, like sign-on bonuses, flexible benefits, and flexible hours and schedules. The salaries are definitely starting to go up as well.

Snell: What are some of the traits of a successful coder?

Prophet: Certainly a good foundation in formal coding education, anatomy and physiology, and medical terminology. Individuals who tend to be very good at coding are very detail-oriented, with perhaps a secret desire to be a detective. That is what it takes, hunting through the medical records looking for medical conditions and procedures that might be buried in there somewhere. A commitment to coding as a career is one thing that we definitely have to foster more. It is not just a job; it really is a career. It takes a commitment to continuing education, to adhering to ethical coding standards, to reading everything you can get your hands on. You need a strong pride in accuracy of work, as well as excellent communication skills to be able to communicate with other departments of the organization and certainly with the physicians.

Snell: What are some of the attributes of an individual that would cause you to believe he or she probably should not go into the coding profession?

Prophet: Disinterest in medical terms or medicine at all. Sloppy work habits. You definitely need to be a perfectionist to be in the coding profession because it is very detail-oriented. Certainly if you want a job in which you're running all over the place and don't want to be sitting at a desk, you would not be right for coding work. Someone who is not very patient and just wants to hurry up and get the chart done, who is more interested in volume completed than in quality would not be appropriate either. Coders need to be thorough.

Snell: If I were looking for a professional coder, how could I increase my chances of finding one?

Prophet: Offer a flexible work schedule. Consider allowing the coding to be done from home. That is becoming popular now. The option of working at home is attractive to a lot of people. Offer good continuing education benefits; coders are pretty savvy about looking at that attribute. Believe it or not, even in this compliance environment, we still hear complaints from coders that they are never allowed to attend any continuing education. If they do want to go to something, they have to pay for it themselves and take a vacation day. That is just horrendous. Offering excellent continuing education opportunities is a good draw. Some organizations are even offering sign-on bonuses.

Snell: Do you think organizations are hiring enough professional coders?

Prophet: It depends on the individual organization. Many are hiring more coders because of coding errors, identified through audits, that were the result of too much focus on productivity and too many records for each coder to manage. Another bad trend that I'm hoping is turning around is assigning a lot of non-coding-related duties to the coding staff. In addition to coding, they have to answer the phone, pull charts for the doctors, or handle release of information requests. More organizations now realize that quality coding means giving coders a private work area and letting them do what they do best, which is code. They see from chart audits that the errors are from lack of time, not a lack of skill or education.

Snell: Some feel that compliance involves a lot more than billing and coding, and that a professional coder can do more to minimize an organization's risk of a large settlement than any other action the organization may take. Do you agree?

Prophet: Yes, definitely. Even though compliance involves a lot more than billing and coding, improper coding can affect a lot of claims, which could result in significant patterns and potentially a very large settlement. Bad coding can have a huge impact, as we have seen in some of the investigations, such as the pneumonia investigation, in which hospitals have been charged with upcoding certain types of pneumonia. Now organizations treat pneumonia patients and code their claims.<AQ> When there is a pattern of upcoding for a fairly common diagnosis, such as pneumonia, the financial impact, in terms of overpayments and penalties, can be staggering. Yes, I think a professional coder can do a great deal to minimize the risk of a large settlement.

Snell: The government is now focusing somewhat on patient care issues. Is there any role for the professional coder in dealing with patient care issues?

Prophet: Yes, the coder actually has a role in a couple of areas. Because of the nature of what coders do, they look at documentation a lot. Obviously, as part of the coding process, they will notice discrepancies in documentation, conflicts between what different health care professionals are saying or between test results and the clinicians' documentation, or some issue that has not been addressed by the physician. Bringing concerns to the physician's attention would certainly improve the overall documentation and, ultimately, improve patient care. Concurrent coding can help because the coders are actually on the nursing units while the patient is still in-house. Pointing out, "Hey, this happened and you didn't address it in your progress notes, and what about the results of this X-ray?" and getting the physician to look at that leads to complete, thorough, accurate documentation while the patient is in-house, and that has a direct impact on patient care.

Complete and accurate coding also reflects the patient's severity of illness. Investigators, auditors, and the department of public health notice when a patient is in the hospital for two weeks and only had one simple, straightforward diagnosis that should typically require only a two- or three-day hospital stay. Often the patient had other complications and comorbidities that were not picked up by the coder. Complete and accurate coding will better reflect the severity of illness, which is then going to match up more closely with patient care and utilization of resources.

Snell: How long do you feel that this compliance phenomenon is going to be the focus of so much attention by the enforcement community?

Prophet: There are two parts to this question. From the enforcement community's perspective, I think it will definitely die down, probably within the next few years. The government's attention may become focused elsewhere, and as compliance becomes more ingrained in every organization, fraud and abuse won't be as much of an issue. But compliance is going to be the focus of the health care provider industry for a very long time—hopefully, forever—as a basic component of operations in the health care environment.

Interview 6

L. Stephan Vincze
Vincze & Frazer, LLC

L. Stephen Vincze is the president and CEO of Vincze & Frazer, LLC. Mr. Vincze brings an extensive background in compliance, and the Office of Inspector General used his draft for the final version of *Compliance Guidance for Third-Party Medical Billing Companies*.

Troklus: Tell me a little about your experiences and what brought you to work in the field of compliance?

Vincze: The son of a physician, I've lived around health care professionals my whole life. A pre-med student in college, I decided early on that chemistry was not for me and that law, political science, and economics captivated my interest. A "conservative contrarian," I bucked the traditional path of my Ivy League classmates of proceeding straight to graduate school and joined the U.S. Marine Corps instead. Commissioned as an artillery officer, I served in the combat arms for three years, from 1982 to 1985, before applying for and being selected for a scholarship to law school through the Marine Corps Funded Law Education Program (FLEP). Elected to the Honor Council by my law school classmates and graduating in 1988, I've been involved in the general field of fraud and abuse prevention and compliance for more than twelve years. After graduating from law school, I was assigned duties that involved advising the base staff judge advocate and commanding general at Parris Island, South Carolina, about environmental, government procurement, and federal military installation compliance. I also served as the counsel to a disciplinary review board of the neighboring Beaufort Naval Hospital. In addition to these duties, I prosecuted and defended criminal cases. Subsequently, I was "tapped" to represent the Marine Corps on a Joint Military Staff in the Office of the Secretary of Defense in the Pentagon. There, I worked as a counsel to the Office of Transition Support and Services and worked closely with the Office of General Counsel and the Office of Legislation and Policy in negotiating and implementing legislation with congressional staff and private insurers that provided for preexisting condition insurance and other health care benefits for military personnel and their families. These successful experiences led to a recommendation to a position as a counsel on defense and military issues to the ranking minority congressman (later the chairman) of the Committee on Government Operations in the U.S. House of Representatives. In this role, I advised the congressional members of the committee with regard to military and defense procurement matters, to include matters involving health care. The committee (now renamed the Government Reform Committee) serves as the principal congressional oversight committee concerned with preventing and stopping government fraud and waste in various executive agencies to include Defense, Justice, and Health and Human Services. The Office of Inspector General of the Department of Health and Human Services regularly testifies before this congressional committee. My role as a counsel involved conducting congressional investigations, developing and preparing congressional hearings, preparing witnesses, writing speeches, etc., on issues that concerned matters of fraud and abuse.

These experiences in the Marine Corps and Capitol Hill, however, served as a prelude to my most direct and core experience with respect to health care compliance. In 1995, the executive management of the largest medical billing company in the country recruited and hired me to design and implement a corporatewide compliance program for their company. This highly successful publicly traded company, the recognized industry leader at the time with over 10,000 employees and 350 offices in all fifty states, had just come under federal investigation in California for alleged billing improprieties two months prior to my arrival. My challenge was to successfully create and implement not only an effective compliance program, but also an industry-leading one that set the standard for medical billing nationwide. My unique mix and combination of experiences as a Marine, a congressional counsel, and a lawyer experienced in federal investigations and fraud and abuse prevention seemed to fit the mold that this health care organization was looking for in its first compliance officer. That is how my career led me into the field of health care compliance.

Troklus: What does the word "compliance" mean to you?

Vincze: Compliance, to me, means doing what is right, not just what is required. Compliance means good business practices. I think all too often the general public hears the word compliance and thinks of it as something negative in connotation and compulsory in tone. But having worked in the field of compliance for a number of years, I think the best meaning of compliance is again, doing what is right, not just what's required, and communicating that concept effectively while developing effective corporate processes for people in an organization with serious questions and concerns. Effective compliance should be focused on operational, proactive, and forward-looking processes as opposed to reactive and defensive explanations. My motto is "Good compliance is good business!" While perhaps a bit redundant, the point is that effective compliance enhances the productivity of business and serves as much more than a mere insurance policy, which is how many executives, managers, and lawyers think of compliance initially. Ideally, an effective compliance program equips an organization to answer or respond to a question or situation that has never been asked or has never occurred before, a situation where no preformulated answer exists in any textbook, a question of first impression. That is the true test of an effective compliance program, in my opinion, and when making "the right decision" is what matters most. Today, businesses of all kinds, but especially health care, create new boundaries and enter new frontiers. An effective compliance program provides a centralized process that harnesses and taps into available resources to address the invariable questions that arise—the tough questions of first impression—that organizations encounter as they compete in these unchartered waters. When issues of public health and safety, public funds, and life and death are involved, as they are in health care, it becomes a "no brainer" that you need every available mechanism and resource available to assist you as an organization to make the best decisions consistently and systematically. Effective compliance programs enable organizations to do that.

Troklus: How many years were you actually a compliance officer or working in a compliance-related area?

Vincze: I worked from August 1995 to May 1997 as a compliance officer in the role that I described earlier, so approximately two years. Since 1997, I have advised a wide variety of health care organizations on compliance matters. My total health care compliance experience is currently about five years. When you combine my non–health care and health care work experiences, I have been professionally involved in some capacity with compliance-related activity for at least twelve years.

Troklus: What did you enjoy most about being a compliance officer?

Vincze: I enjoyed communicating with employees and management while conducting training sessions. I felt that, as a compliance officer, I held a unique role as an executive that served as a bridge between executives and employees. This unique and independent position enabled me to effect positive change within a complex organization that was "under fire." I enjoyed creating something new—a new department, a new process, that I believed, and strongly believe now, had a positive impact on the company. It strengthened the company from both a legal perspective—ensuring problems were properly addressed sooner rather than later through a systematic process—and an operational perspective—enhancing the quality of services and leading to a more competitive position. The compliance program and my role as a compliance officer enhanced the spirit of teamwork and leadership within the company, by linking the concept of teamwork and communication with individual and corporate productivity and advancement. It helped foster what is referred to in the Marine Corps as "esprit de corps." I felt the most rewarding part of being a compliance officer was working with the different people in the company and having the opportunity to interact with them in a manner that encouraged and produced positive change through teamwork and communication.

Troklus: Did you feel that as a compliance officer you had greater liability than anyone else working in an administrative health care position?

Vincze: The short answer is "No." I think senior executives, leaders in any organization, are accountable for good results and for bad results within their areas of responsibility. So, I think when you are an executive in a company, you should accept that responsibility of leadership. That is not to suggest that there aren't differences between the responsibilities of a compliance officer and other executives. As a compliance officer you have little if any control over executive decisions. You act as the "squeaky wheel," ensuring that your voice is heard by the key decision makers. A compliance officer acts as a facilitator and communicator who ensures that senior management and the board have the necessary information to make appropriate decisions and take appropriate actions with regard to compliance matters. Generally speaking, a compliance officer does not make key management decisions or take management actions. Nevertheless, given the potential ramifications of compliance issues, a compliance officer certainly has the potential of being seen as more on the front lines, so to speak. There's also a real "shoot the messenger" syndrome where the compliance officer is often the target. Let's face it, a compliance officer is not necessarily everyone's favorite person when he or she shows up, especially in the beginning before people fully understand or appreciate the role of a compliance officer. Most people assume a compliance officer is like "Big Brother" or the "corporate cop" who is looking for only problems and trouble. But a general counsel often encounters similar situations; and of course, a CEO is front and center when it comes to liability—"the buck stops at the top." Overall, my answer would be no, I don't believe compliance officers are at any greater risk than other executives, but let me be clear—there certainly are risks to consider before being a compliance officer and these risks may differ from those of other senior executive positions.

Troklus: Do you advise compliance officers to obtain liability insurance?

Vincze: I have not advised any compliance officers to do that yet. When I was a compliance officer, such liability insurance did not exist to the best of my knowledge. I think it is a relatively recent development from insurance companies. I have read and have heard from compliance officers that increasingly they harbor concerns of personal liability and of the potential of being a "scapegoat" if anything goes wrong in their organization. That is a realistic issue to confront and to consider when one chooses to become a compliance officer. I am not sure that liability insurance would necessarily protect a compliance officer, so I do not currently recommend it per se, but I would keep an open mind about it.

Troklus: You are now a consultant. What role do you feel that a consultant plays in compliance?

Vincze: The role of a consultant is to "add value" to an organization. A consultant's ability to do so often depends on the type of organization that is involved and its current compliance needs—for some organizations, there is no role for a consultant; for others, there is an essential role for one.

I think a quality consultant will advise any organization that is considering his or her services how best to employ that consultant's skills, if at all. I have played numerous different roles within organizations depending on their specific compliance needs. Some organizations that I have dealt with more recently have already developed their compliance programs. They've had them in place for some time and would like an independent, objective review of the strengths and weaknesses of their program. I have been fortunate to be surrounded by an exceptional team of highly skilled and experienced health care professionals in our firm who are well qualified to conduct such a review. The key constant that I emphasize to compliance officers and other professionals who may consider our services is that effective compliance hinges on credibility—credibility of the program, credibility of the processes developed, credibility of the policies and procedures implemented, and credibility of the people involved. Part of that credibility is how regularly a program is evaluated and by whom. I would suggest that a consultant can play a valuable role in being an independent, objective reviewer to ensure a compliance program stays on track and is responsive to the internal operational needs of the organization as well as the external regulatory expectations of the government.

Another important and valuable role that a consultant can offer is that of a mentor to a compliance officer. Often, particularly with organizations that are just starting their compliance program, numerous situations arise when it is useful and prudent to have available a second opinion from a seasoned and experienced professional who has worked with the government and with other health care organizations on developing and implementing effective compliance programs. There is tremendous value in not "reinventing the wheel" and to have available at your fingertips a respected outside authority who can "play the heavy," if necessary, to break an internal deadlock or to explain to a compliance committee, for example, the merits of a certain course of action. I have played such a role with a number of different organizations and compliance officers. I found it useful when I was a compliance officer to have available such an advisor and mentor.

Finally, I would suggest that an experienced and knowledgeable consultant can save tremendous time and money for an organization by accurately identifying what existing resources and mechanisms can be utilized to build or enhance a compliance program. Again, such a role saves an organization from reinventing the wheel. An effective consultant can marshal information that they have accumulated from their cumulative experiences and apply it as needed to help an organization start a new program or to improve an existing one in a credible, quality, and cost-effective manner.

Troklus: What similarities do you see when comparing the health care compliance initiatives to those of the Department of Defense?

Vincze: For one thing, both industries were under fire and in the public limelight for having problems with fraud and abuse. Also, both industries involved large amounts of public funds from the U.S. government—in health care for Medicare/Medicaid and Tri-Care (formerly called CHAMPUS) and in defense for support of the military and its operational requirements, especially weapon systems. So, in both health care and in defense there is a high level of fiscal responsibility for taxpayer funds that creates an impetus and need for government oversight. This government oversight in turn puts pressure on the private sector—in the defense industry, defense contractors felt the oversight glare, and in health care, it is providers and other organizations that receive payment through government programs that come under the watchful eye of government regulators. Other similarities are that within both industries there are at least

pockets, if not large segments, of skepticism as to exactly what a compliance program is and what it can achieve. However, on a positive note, I have also seen growing acceptance and understanding of the positive benefits of an effective compliance program as the health care compliance initiatives have evolved over the past few years. Earlier I alluded to building esprit de corps as a positive benefit of a compliance program. The defense industry is a good model in this regard because its experience has shown that progressing to a business ethics rather than a pure legal compliance program achieves greater "buy-in" and acceptance of a compliance program by the people you want to use it—everyone in the organization. I find that employees both in defense and health care are more motivated and willing to embrace a program that is centered on the concept of doing what is right and is not just concerned with abiding by the letter of the law. Certainly, employees and managers need to be aware of legal and regulatory requirements. However, in terms of instilling and maintaining support and continued effectiveness for a compliance program, studies have shown that linking legal compliance to an ethical decision-making framework is most effective. The defense industry's compliance programs have evolved in that manner, and I see a similar evolution in health care compliance programs as well.

Troklus: What are differences between health care and the Department of Defense compliance initiatives?

Vincze: One of the key and fundamental differences between the defense and health care industries is the significantly greater complexity of the health care industry relative to the defense industry. The defense industry players essentially formed a triangle consisting of Congress, the Department of Defense department, and the private defense companies and consultants—the General Dynamics, the Lockheeds, and the Boeings of the world. Health care, however, is much more fragmented, with multiple players such as managed care organizations, hospitals, physician provider groups, and the various support organizations such as laboratories, durable medical equipment companies, and medical billing companies. And, of course, who could forget the public's favorite—the insurance carriers and fiscal intermediaries. So health care is clearly a much more complex system to regulate and oversee. Consequently, it is much more difficult to gain consensus on what system and what results equate to effective compliance. That is why I think you see various compliance guidelines addressing various sectors of the health care industry issued by the Office of Inspector General. With the defense industry, there was just one defense initiative. It wasn't parceled out between different sectors because there weren't different sectors to address. The relative complexity of health care to defense is the key difference between the two industries in my opinion.

Troklus: What is your opinion of the model guidance for compliance programs being issued by the Office of Inspector General?

Vincze: By and large, they have been excellent. I am a strong supporter of the guidances that have been issued by the Office of Inspector General. That is not to say that I agree with every word that has been written in them, but the guidances have served an extremely positive role—to provide significantly greater clarity and precision to the private sector's understanding of the expectations of the Office of Inspector General regarding the necessary component parts of effective compliance programs and some of the specific risks they should be designed to address. The Office of Inspector General deserves a lot of credit—overall, they have served the health care industry and the needs of the public well by issuing these guidances.

Troklus: You submitted a draft compliance billing guidance to the Office of Inspector General. What were your biggest challenges in developing that draft?

Vincze: My biggest challenges involved building the necessary political consensus and support, first within the billing industry and then within the OIG, to overcome strongly held mutual suspicions between these public and private sector groups. Breaking down the barriers that these suspicions created and then focusing on the substantive tasks and the mutually shared objective of preventing fraud and abuse proved both challenging and rewarding. "The politics of partnership," as I refer to the process we used, is what I strongly advocated and employed to address this situation. I essentially employed on a macro-level the same process I used on a micro-level within the company that hired me to put together its corporate compliance program. I merely expanded the consensus-building process I had successfully learned and employed in my "trials by fire" at the Pentagon, on Capitol Hill, and in the corporate world to an industrywide level. Working at such a level, therefore, necessitated working with and through an organization that could credibly claim to represent the industry. That organization was the International Billing Association [IBA], now renamed the Healthcare Billing and Management Association [HBMA]. Again, gaining consensus first within the industry, and second, between the industry and the Office of Inspector General, were the biggest challenges and the biggest rewards once we succeeded; and we did! To gain consensus, you must have participation of representative people with different perspectives. We formed a committee within the association of billing companies that consisted of various types of companies—large to small, privately owned, publicly traded, etc.—and tried to identify with precision their concerns and the kinds of compliance risks and issues they felt needed to be addressed by a prospective compliance guidance from the government. Once that was achieved, we needed to build consensus with the Office of Inspector General general counsel's office to ensure that they understood why the industry recommended what it did. Initially, the billing industry was reluctant to engage in this endeavor, and many billers held the view of "Why should we even suggest what we want to the Office of Inspector General? Let's just stay out of this." I suggested that if the industry did not partner with the government, then the government may create onerous compliance requirements simply because they may not understand the nuances of the industry as well as the industry did. A key concept and major breakthrough was persuading representatives of the billing industry that the government shared their fundamental issue of concern—stopping and preventing fraudulent billing while maintaining viable and profitable billing operations. Representatives from the industry and the OIG deserve a lot of credit for working together to achieve a common understanding about a shared objective.

Troklus: Was your draft used in the creation of the OIG's guidance?

Vincze: Yes, that is my understanding. However, I want to make sure that people understand that while I hammered out the initial draft of the proposed guidance on my computer keyboard and that this draft was largely accepted by the association and submitted to the OIG for consideration, I certainly was not alone in making a significant contribution to the overall effort that concluded with the issuance of the OIG guidance for medical billing companies. Members of the association's Compliance and Ethics Committee worked diligently on that draft and improved it. The entire association submitted that revised draft to the Office of Inspector General, and the OIG did in fact use it as the principal source to issue the guidance. The OIG made several changes (some of which we objected to strenuously), but they also incorporated other whole sections verbatim. By and large, the experience reinforced my belief that when it comes to fraud and abuse prevention and compliance, the politics of partnership that I have consistently advocated works.

Troklus: What influence do you feel the third-party billing guidance will have on the "new" physician practice guidance? Do you think there will be many similarities? If so, what do you see being duplicated?

Vincze: A little background history may be helpful on this point. Before announcing the issuance of the new physician compliance guidance, the Office of Inspector General had announced that physicians looking for guidance for compliance program development/implementation should look to the third-party medical billing guidance. The OIG originally did not intend to release separate guidance for physicians. When you think about it, it makes a lot of sense because the billing issues essentially remain the same whether you bill yourself as a physician or if you outsource it to a third-party billing company. The coding and documentation requirements and the safeguards to ensure proper billing are the same; it is just a question of who does them. One of the things that the third-party medical billing guidance did that was unique, was to specifically address how to coordinate between providers, in terms of individual and mutual compliance responsibilities. The guidance recommends that providers and billers coordinate their compliance responsibilities contractually. My sense in working with the health care industry is that, despite all the guidances for different sectors like hospitals and managed care organizations, people are still finding that physicians are reluctant to accept their compliance responsibilities unless they hear it directly from a credible governmental authority; they simply don't want to be bothered by what many of them see as governmental interference and administrative red tape. This difficulty in persuading physicians to adopt their own compliance programs is, I believe, in large part, the impetus behind the issuance of guidance for physicians separately. It is a bit ironic that some physicians and groups that represent physicians requested this guidance. I was surprised initially, because having grown up with a father who is a physician and working with physicians closely, I think if you ask them directly, "Do you want more guidance from the government?" their answer probably is going to be not only "No!" but "Hell no!" At the same time, the government is in a sort of Catch-22 situation—if it doesn't give guidance, people complain that they don't know what is expected of them, and if it does give guidance, then people are upset about government intrusion and interference. I can respect and empathize with both the physicians' perspective—they went to medical school to learn how to treat and heal sick people not to fill out forms—and the government's position—it has a fiscal responsibility that public funds are appropriately spent only on authorized procedures. My sense is that the new physician compliance guidance will address more practical and logistical issues. For example, in a small physician practice it may not be feasible to hire a senior executive as a compliance officer. As I understand it, the physician guidance will address that issue and perhaps suggest the possibility of using one compliance officer for several group practices in a kind of pooling arrangement. In terms of current billing issues, I really don't see many differences from the previous billing guidance that may emerge. We will have to wait and see. Regardless, I have heard from the OIG that it will continue to recommend that the new physician guidance be used in conjunction with the third-party medical billing guidance. Using both guidances would be the best way for a physician practice to be prepared.

Troklus: Should a physician practice that is considering contracting with a billing company ask for a copy of its compliance plan or program?

Vincze: Absolutely. I would say that in today's world it borders on negligence for any physician group or any lawyer representing a physician group not to make "Do you have a compliance program? If you do, we would like to see a copy of it" a standard question and request for a billing company under consideration.

Troklus: If a billing company does not have a compliance plan or program, should that immediately alert the physician to shop elsewhere?

Vincze: It should send up a warning flag. I wouldn't necessarily say the physician should go elsewhere, but I think the next question to the billing company should be whether the billing company is working toward implementing a compliance program. If so, what is the estimated time frame for implementation and what will the compliance program consist of when implemented? This would give the billing company the opportunity to demonstrate that it is, in fact, taking due diligent steps to implement an effective compliance program. It is prudent, regardless of whether the billing company has a compliance program, to look at the different options available from different billing companies. I would suggest that the mere fact that a billing company has a compliance program, in itself, is not sufficient either. Again, you want to make sure that the plan or program is a real one, one that is being followed and does not exist just on paper. I would caution people not to be too hasty in judgments based purely on an answer of "Yes" or "No" to the question of "Do you have a compliance plan/program?" One should verify that it is a program that exists in day-to-day practice and not just on paper or cyberspace.

Troklus: What are two indicators of a billing compliance program's effectiveness?

Vincze: First, are all of the employees aware of the compliance program? That is one of the key things that government investigators look for. They go into a company and randomly ask people, "Tell me about your code of conduct. Tell me about your hotline. Tell me about your compliance program. Who is your compliance officer?" If the employees don't know the answers to those questions and stare blankly into space, that is a warning that the compliance program may not be effective or real. Employees need to be aware of the compliance program in order to follow it. Again, employee awareness of the compliance program and its component parts is one key indicator.

Another key test is what the company has done, and what actions it has taken in response to problems identified by its compliance program. This may be a sensitive area that companies may not want to discuss with outsiders, but under certain circumstances (with appropriate attorney-client privilege), this information may be shared. Taking appropriate organizational action in light of verified improper conduct is a key test of compliance program effectiveness. Ultimately, what counts most is what you do, how you respond to an identified problem. If you find problems, or people report problems, and nothing is done about them, then the compliance program is not serving its purpose, which is to diligently identify, correct, and prevent misconduct and fraud and abuse. I would say that the two key indicators of compliance program effectiveness are: (1) "Are people aware of the compliance program?"; and (2) "Are they using it and is the company taking action to correct problems that it identifies?"

Troklus: What do you see as the top three benefits of having an effective compliance program?

Vincze: The three core benefits of a compliance program are (1) liability protection, (2) operational quality enhancement, and (3) improved organizational competitiveness. Through effective compliance you attain enhanced communications among employees, managers, and supervisors. You identify problems sooner rather than later. That not only serves to reduce your exposure to liability, but also serves to create enhancements in your operations. Finally, that enhancement of operations should give organizations a competitive advantage. For example, in terms of reimbursement, we have found that as people document more accurately and more precisely, their reimbursement levels tend to increase. That is because the more precisely you document, the more likely you are to assign a more specific code. We find that effective compliance leads to positive business results. It also translates into better patient care. As physicians and other health care professionals document more accurately and precisely what care was provided and why, a more accurate historical record of patient care exists. Doctors can then refer to these records and make better, more informed patient care decisions. Overall, I would summarize by saying the top three benefits of an effective compliance program are (1) liability protection, (2) improved operational quality, and (3) a competitive advantage in the marketplace.

Troklus: What are the risk areas that billing services should look out for?

Vincze: This is a rather long list, and I would refer people to the list that's in the OIG guidance for third-party medical billing companies. To highlight some of the top three that come to mind, I would focus on improper documentation or lack of sufficient documentation of providers that shows the actual services billed were in fact rendered and that sufficient medical necessity existed to qualify for reimbursement. This first issue is related to the next issue, which is improper coding such as "upcoding" (assigning a code that inappropriately reimburses the provider at a level higher than was warranted according to the service documented) and "assumption coding" (assigning a diagnosis code based on the procedure performed without supporting documentation in the medical record, e.g., assigning a code for pneumonia for a chest x-ray without any other information). Finally, the third top issue that is increasingly moving to the forefront with the use of the Internet and electronic media is confidentiality of medical records and patient information. Patients are rightfully concerned about the privacy and confidentiality of their medical records. Congress and the president are increasingly considering imposing severe criminal penalties for breaches in this area. Health care professionals need to be very cognizant of this issue and take appropriate safeguards when they are handling the medical records of patients.

Troklus: If a problem is found, how far back would you look?

Vincze: The recommendation of attorneys and of people in the government is that you should look as far back as the statute of limitations, which is generally six years. It also depends on the nature of the problem. One problem that often comes up is the issue of credit balances, when organizations find that they have credits on their books to which they are not entitled. For whatever reason, they have been overcompensated. They have tried to repay it, but it hasn't been accepted. That is an issue that needs to be looked at carefully. In that case, you may have a fairly sizable credit balance that may be affected. It is also important to keep in mind that your local and state laws may be implicated in that time frame.

Troklus: What is the difference between a simple billing error and fraud?

Vincze: Essentially, it comes down to one word—a pattern. A simple billing error is not a pattern of continued errors. You can have fraud and not have a specific intent to defraud, but rather have a reckless disregard for the circumstances. A repeated error, for example, would be the assignment of a 25 modifier to a bill, which may not be warranted by existing documentation. You may have a software program that automatically makes such an assignment erroneously due to a programming error. If it does it for hundreds and even thousands of claims time after time, and you fail to catch it because you have failed to implement appropriate quality controls or some kind of checking mechanism and just assume everything is working fine, then arguably that inaction and the resultant pattern of improper billing could be construed as reckless disregard of the circumstances and be fraud. This argument is especially compelling in light of all the discussions, warnings, and materials in the industry that advise about the importance and necessity of proper documentation and quality controls. In contrast, you may have implemented a compliance program that properly trains your employees on appropriate policies and procedures that require proper documentation. You become aware however, that one person, a clerk, who for whatever reason did not follow the appropriate policy and procedure and assigned an incorrect modifier (perhaps a physician called and persuaded her to do so). But you catch the error or it is brought to your attention by the carrier. That was one error that can be corrected. Hopefully, your compliance program would detect that error. And the key after detection is correction and prevention. Again, the key difference between a billing error and fraud is a pattern of repeated mistakes over time; fraud has a pattern, errors do not.

Troklus: What is your opinion on voluntary disclosure?

Vincze: Through the Office of Inspector General, voluntary disclosure has evolved positively over the past few years. The initial voluntary disclosure program or protocol that was issued was not successful in achieving its goal, namely, to encourage large numbers of people and organizations to voluntarily "turn themselves in." I believe a total of twelve or at least less than twenty disclosures were made over a two-year period. The principal reason for the failure of the initial program, I believe, is that it did not create sufficient incentives for people to come forward to disclose concerns with their organizations. Today, that has changed. I recommend to organizations that disclosure is something that should be seriously considered and followed if the circumstances are correct. One of the misconceptions about voluntary disclosure is that whenever you find anything of concern, you have to go directly to the Office of Inspector General or the U.S. attorney. That is not the case. The OIG's own guidance on this issue specifically points out that, unless there is specific evidence of criminal violation of the law with the requisite intent, the first level you should go to is the local regional carrier or fiscal intermediary. This often surprises people.

The other key point that I would make about voluntary disclosure is that to have a successful outcome from voluntary disclosure, credibility is the key. The credibility of any consultants or people you have externally assisting your organization in the voluntary disclosure process is critically important. According to feedback I have received, our clients who have engaged in the voluntary disclosure process have been successful because of their efforts, their forthrightness, the quality of their compliance programs, and the people they had working on their disclosures. Some old-school hospital or health care administrators prefer a minimalist response, i.e., send a check for the overpayment with a short one-paragraph cover letter. It has been my experience that such a disclosure heightens the suspicion of the carrier and may lead to a referral to the OIG for further investigation. A much wiser and effective course of action is to explain thoroughly what the facts and circumstances are that led to the disclosure and who, what, when, how, and why did the organization respond. I have found that such a disclosure reinforces or establishes a very credible position and has been accepted without further inquiry in every case. Again, credibility is the key to a successful outcome.

Voluntary disclosure, however, should not be jumped into without some careful research. Before you make any voluntary disclosure, the first thing to do is to find out what circumstances you face. Get the facts about your own internal situation and know how bad or how good things are before you make any decision about disclosing. At the same time, disclosure should *not* be something that is feared and avoided at all costs. It is a process that should be used prudently under the appropriate circumstances. When to disclose, to whom, and how are the key issues to address and ones that an experienced professional who's been through it before can help you answer correctly. This is one area in particular where there is little room for error and "winging it" makes no sense.

Troklus: I know there are several small billing entities across the country. What do you think of sharing a compliance officer among several small entities?

Vincze: Sharing a compliance officer is a relatively new and novel concept. This concept, however, has been applied historically in other situations in the legal world. The whole idea of circuit judges is based on a similar concept where a judge is shared among different communities because there just aren't enough to go around. In terms of efficiency, it makes sense. There are pros and cons to this, however. I advise people to be cautious. Ideally, if you can afford it, it's always best to have your own compliance officer. With a small entity, however, such as a small physician group practice, that just may not be economically feasible. I think sharing a compliance officer can work. Here is what I would recommend to organizations that are considering this: Make sure that the shared compliance officer has the credentials, the background, the training, the experience, the personality, and the physical availability to be effective for you. Compliance officers need to have a number of different traits besides just knowledge of the rules and regulations. They need to be effective leaders, spokespersons, communicators, and have a strong backbone to point out when things are wrong and also to take the heat from the "shoot the messenger" syndrome I alluded to earlier. It is very important to pick the right person to ensure that there is a quality compliance professional with a regular physical presence in your organization.

Troklus: What words of wisdom do you have for billing companies that are in the process of implementing compliance programs?

Vincze: First, start now! I really believe that billing companies that do not have compliance programs of any kind will eventually be forced out of business. If you think of compliance as a quality, operational enhancement process that improves what you do, then you can see how companies that employ compliance will attract more and more clients, and rightfully so. Second, ensure that you do it right. One of the great developments over the past five years has been the recognition by the Office of Inspector General and the government that it does take time to implement a quality compliance program. I recall a senior official in the Office of Inspector General explaining that what they look for in a compliance program is consistent documented progress in compliance program development and implementation. Don't worry that you have to do it overnight. If you do that, chances are that you won't have a good program. Be diligent, be expeditious about it, but also be careful and do it right.

Also, I would stress that you should get input from your employees. Involve your organization in the development; don't just force-feed something down their throats. The best compliance program is one that reflects the unique business culture and mix of compliance risks of a particular organization. The only way to successfully customize a compliance program in this way is to ensure your employees participate in the development of the program.

Troklus: Where do you see compliance in the next five years?

Vincze: This is an interesting question, particularly for me since I have been involved in health care compliance for approximately five years. To see the changes that have occurred between 1995 and 2000 is really remarkable. I don't have a crystal ball, but the first thing I would say is that compliance is here to stay. By compliance, I mean health care organizations maintaining management processes to prevent and detect fraud and abuse and illegal conduct. Compliance is not a fad that may disappear like various management programs that have come and gone over the years. The reason for this difference between popular management programs and compliance is that compliance has specific legal consequences and penalties associated with it. That really forces organizations to pay attention to the government's guidance and implement compliance programs. The government has conducted a "crackdown"—their words, not mine—and the government enforcement efforts have had rather dramatic results. As long as the government continues to exact large penalties and fines, recoups significant settlement agreements, and continues to find fraud and abuse, compliance will be here for some time. As I mentioned earlier, I think we will see an evolution in health care as we have seen in the defense industry toward an ethics-based program that is focused on doing what is right, not just what is required. The other thing I see in the future is the expansion of our own domestic health care compliance initiatives internationally. I see health care compliance going global. I have already seen a company in India processing health care bills for American companies. I think that is just the beginning. Ed Mendoza, M.D., M.B.A., who is affiliated with our firm has written perhaps the most comprehensive work on international health care systems to date. He suggests that a number of countries are employing the Diagnostic Related Group (DRG)–based billing system that our country developed in the 1980s. Once that happens, the next question is, "How do you police it?" The bottom line is that in five years, I see at least the beginning of the internationalization of health care compliance, particularly in English-speaking countries like Canada, Australia, and the United Kingdom. Ultimately, other countries will realize the economic, i.e., bottom-line, good business benefits that effective compliance programs and processes produce. The message that "Good compliance is good business!" will translate well in other languages and cultures as countries continue to evolve and grow their democratic political institutions in conjunction with their capitalistic economic systems. Fraud is a worldwide problem and has negative economic effects everywhere. To the degree compliance programs can effectively combat fraud and produce positive economic results, they will be adopted by other countries in the future.

Interview 7

Sheryl Vacca
Sutter Health

Sheryl Vacca is director of the West Coast Compliance Practice for Deloitte & Touche, LLP. Her prior experience as corporate compliance officer at Sutter Health provides the large system perspective.

Troklus: What health care background do you bring to your position as compliance officer?

Vacca: I have a bachelor of science degree in nursing and a master's of science degree in administration. I have been working in health care for twenty-three years, from bedside nursing to various administrative positions. Compliance officer became my role five years ago. At that time, this also included supporting the system's governing boards, of which there were approximately fifty-three, and overseeing two outpatient clinics in the Sacramento area. In addition, internal audit became another area of my responsibility. Licensing, regulatory, and accreditation aspects of different health care businesses has been a focus throughout my career, which has been useful in the compliance arena. So I have actually been working in the compliance field for at least the last ten years, although it wasn't always called compliance.

Troklus: Coming from a nursing background, how do you feel quality of care issues play into the compliance picture?

Vacca: Quality of care issues have a huge impact on compliance, especially with the application of the False Claims Act to some of these issues. If the government detects inadequate quality or if the facility breaks a quality regulation, i.e., infraction of EMTALA, the government feels you should not get reimbursement for care which did not meet the standard of care. This substandard can result in application of the False Claims Act. I think the government's role in addressing quality of care should be limited because of an overall lack of understanding of all the aspects of what "quality" really means. In fact, the health care industry has a problem measuring quality. The industry doesn't want any bad outcomes, but there are still different ideas about the definition of quality and what universal standards of care should be.

It is apparent that the government's focus on quality is overlapping with the compliance area. I see the government starting to at least hold the industry accountable for the basic quality standard that we say we provide when it comes to a specific type of care, for instance, in nursing home or home health. I don't disagree that there are problems in those arenas; I also think that the government needs to take into consideration that part of those problems are related to the fact that, to operate the business, more resources are needed in regard to payment systems for those services. Part of the reason that we're where we are with some of the quality issues is because of decreased support associated with the government's payment systems, which have changed over the years. The industry has tried to respond to fewer resources and still offer the same quality, but unfortunately, it is difficult to be successful and continue to provide a high standard of quality care.

Troklus: What background, experience, and/or credentials do you think are important or necessary for a compliance officer to have?

Vacca: I think compliance officers' backgrounds should be related to the operation to which they are providing oversight. This is a very complex industry, and therefore it can be difficult to understand the complexities of how business becomes compliance issues. Having familiarity with the respective operation assists this understanding to work with employees at all levels. Good interpersonal and organizational skills are necessary. Usually this position has no authority, so you must be able to get the job done through a high degree of influence. To be able to influence, the compliance officer must be respected and have credibility with all employees. A compliance officer also should have an ability to facilitate change. Since the role usually has no authority to steer the organization in a particular direction, you want to be able to assist individuals to identify and resolve compliance issues. Doing so will be good for business, providing an environment of "doing the right thing" for their employees, and good for them individually.

Compliance officers also should be personable. It is difficult for compliance officers who position themselves in their office to be very effective; visibility is absolutely critical to the role. The individual needs to be able to get out and work among the employees. This will assist him or her in understanding the complex business issues and provide the employees direct access to the compliance officer. Compliance officers also need to be able to solve problems and participate in high-level decision making. When you open up your compliance office, issues come from every avenue in the business. While you may not be an expert in all aspects of the health care business, you need to at least be able to triage the issues. Compliance officers especially need to know when to direct issues to legal counsel for further investigation and resolution versus when to handle them on an in-house lower level (problems with system or logistics). Compliance officers also find themselves in positions where, politically, some management will use compliance to effect change in a management capacity that they could not do without compliance. An example would be where a manager is investigated under compliance because the senior manager was not able to do an investigation under his or her own direction because of a strong political environment. Compliance officers need to have some intuition and skill to manage that situation and others in the political culture of their business. They want to make sure that they are not manipulated to get something accomplished under the guise of compliance that management hasn't been able to accomplish otherwise due to politics or lack of action.

Troklus: How were you involved in implementing the compliance program at Sutter Health?

Vacca: I have been here since the inception of our corporate compliance program. Initially I worked with one of our associate legal counsels, and we coteamed to develop the program. Legal input was important. However, the actual implementation and development of our compliance program required more than the legal perspective. It was important for the

system and for our CEO that our compliance program not be legal-driven. However, my knowledge regarding the legal aspects of a compliance program was at a deficit, so we used our internal legal resources to get us started. After a period of time of a ninety-degree learning curve, I took the lead on further development and implementation of our program. Our legal counsel still continues to be involved through their advice and with necessary areas of investigation.

Troklus: As compliance officer at Sutter Health, what do you find exciting about the position?

Vacca: The learning curve is continuous. You cannot possibly know every business aspect of an organization this size. It is exciting and challenging because almost every day I find a new area in which I need to develop at least some general knowledge. As we continue in the area to identify problems and bring them to resolution, my knowledge naturally increases. In addition, it's challenging, in that no rock gets turned over without finding something that can be improved. It's rewarding to watch as the organization's culture changes or becomes positively enhanced, the employees become more aware, and they actually start to take ownership for the kinds of things that you worked diligently to bring to their attention. It is especially rewarding when someone actually asks a question before implementing the business aspect, instead of going into the business aspect and then calling and asking, "Did we do this wrong?"

I am concerned that our industry may potentially label compliance officers as potential whistle blowers. I think that we have to be very careful about how we go forward. In addition to that, I think the challenge still remains to exert influence without authority, especially when you are in the position for more than three years. It is difficult, when the organization is attuned to the bottom line and trying to survive, to bring up a compliance issue that you know is going to "break the bank." That is a hard stand to take, but we all want to be good corporate citizens and you have to fix the problem, regardless of cost.

Troklus: How would you define the term "effectiveness"? What would you consider as the three essential elements of an effective compliance program?

Vacca: Effectiveness is when outcome measurements identify that you have achieved compliance. One essential element of effectiveness is, of course, ownership and buy-in from all levels of the organization, particularly from the top. A second element is that generally employees know where to take issues or concerns and know who the CO[1] is. Probably the third element is maintaining your program with the necessary resources to proactively identify areas that may become issues for you, correct the areas that are issues for you, and ensure that they don't reoccur.

Troklus: Measuring a compliance program's effectiveness can be quite a challenge. How would you suggest beginning the process?

Vacca: Regardless of the size of your institution, there are fundamental elements involved in measuring your compliance effectiveness. First, you have to have your framework in place, and then you want to measure whether your framework is actually operating successfully as planned. For

---

[1] compliance officer

instance, you want to ensure compliance to the policies and procedures so you develop measurement tools to complement them. All seven elements of the sentencing guidelines should have an associated measurement method. I would start by getting my framework in place and then measure each of the elements to ensure that, at least on a peripheral basis, they are achieving the desired outcomes. As soon as your program has been around a long enough time to gain credibility, more substantive issues will begin to come forward. More advanced measurement tools to look at effectiveness will need to be developed. I don't advocate one standard method; I think there are many methods to measure effectiveness. Outcome-oriented measurements are important. Ask, "What difference did this process make? Was there value added because our proactive audit identified a potential or real compliance issue? Is the training being performed really decreasing or helping to prevent compliance issues? Are you looking at key high-risk areas that the government has identified for us already? Are there other high-risk areas you need to look at?" These questions and their answers will seem overwhelming, but measurement in these areas will evolve with your compliance program. Again, the first step is measuring whether the framework that you developed is actually doing what you say it is supposed to do. Do your staff know how to raise a concern? Are the issues being resolved and not reoccurring? Does the board and senior management know about the compliance program?

Troklus: So much of what a compliance officer does is hard to measure. Do you feel that effectiveness measures should be quantitative?

Vacca: That's a good question. Again, you are very process-oriented when you first start. If I were to look at quantitative measurement, it would mean volume of high-risk issues, was there repayment, self-disclosure, and/or how do I compare to a baseline audit that was done with employees or risk areas initially? Amount of dollars returned to the government is not a substantial measurement of our compliance program's effectiveness. I think the program's effectiveness comes more from keeping something from becoming a compliance issue, and making sure that those issues that were identified were quickly resolved and were not repeated. Or looking at how successful you were in your measures of effectiveness that hopefully prevented corporate integrity agreements. Those are the kinds of outcomes I look for to judge my effectiveness. I also look to see that I am visible in our system, and that people know where they are supposed to go if they have compliance issues. I try to be as visible as I possibly can be to the organization, even though it is very large. I think my effectiveness also is measured by ensuring retribution is identified and quickly handled. If there is retribution, then I think it is my responsibility to ensure that this is handled by the appropriate chain of command and that employees do not have to deal with repercussions or further threat of retribution.

Troklus: If an effectiveness standard were available, do you feel it would make the job of compliance officer more focused?

Vacca: Yes, I believe that if we had standard measurements that everybody agreed to—just as we have the seven elements of the sentencing guidelines—it would be much easier to articulate the requirements to your board and senior leadership. If each element of an effective compliance program were more defined in standards of effectivness, it would be much easier to convey what needs to be done in a compliance program. It is really difficult now to talk about compliance; even though the government thinks it is pretty black and white, it really isn't. Identifying your role to others or discussing the elements of a compliance program really is hard. Constituents of your organization have difficulty understanding what the program is and why it is necessary when there are no real benchmarks for effectiveness standards except those you can take from the corporate integrity agreements. Understanding the role becomes clearer when you become involved in resolving the compliance issue.

Troklus: Since interviewing employees can give insight as to how your program is doing, if you were given the ability to ask general compliance questions to employees in the hall, what would your number one question be?

Vacca: I think my number one question would be, "What happens when you have a concern or an issue that you think relates to compliance? Do you know what to do with that?"

Troklus: What does the term "broadening your compliance program" mean to you?

Vacca: When you first start out, the first things you think about are your volume of issues and the types of calls you receive on your hotline. You know human resources issues are going to be the majority of your calls so you monitor this as it evolves. As your program reaches your second year, the issues in compliance broaden. It goes beyond the obvious human resources issues and begins to involve more billing issues and other aspects of business, i.e., contracts, etc. To me, broadening is getting into those little niches that you never really would have related to compliance, such as, for instance, quality. How does quality really relate to compliance? In developing your look at quality, how are you going to help people understand why the CO's nose should be in their business of taking care of patients? How will you be able to integrate your focus with current operations and quality? Broadening is looking at contracts and setting up a structure that identifies completely that you have addressed every issue that there would be in both contract development and implementation. Broadening is setting the direction for the future. It is identifying that the benefits of a compliance program are good for the organization and for your public beneficiaries. You are helping them recognize that we are a compliant industry. We do the best that we can with the complexities related to our industry. In the audiences that I get the chance to discuss this with, I reiterate that compliance isn't black and white. It's beyond that. Broadening is moving into e-commerce and moving into all the different aspects related to intellectual property, HIPAA[2] and all the elements of electronic information, i.e., security, privacy, and confidentiality. It's actually taking advantage of our intellectual resources and developing them further. Broadening is moving to a different dimension in compliance programs, especially as our compliance programs mature and have existed beyond a few years. We need to lead the evolution of compliance programs in our industry, not be led by the government.

Troklus: When one is considering the expansion of a compliance program, what key issues should be considered?

Vacca: To begin with, I think you have to consider what your different departments are doing within your organization. One of the key areas that becomes really problematic for a compliance program is if it sits parallel, for instance, to a risk management department. Risk management departments are very clear on their areas of responsibility and oversight. Your

---

[2]Health Insurance Portability and Accountability Act

success will depend on how well those people see you as a partner and a collaborator rather than as a threat that you are moving into their territory. Helping legal departments understand that there is more to a compliance issue than the legal aspects can be a difficult task. Legal aspects are often accompanied with operational issues, and legal and compliance have to work together toward a resolution. I think that is the biggest challenge when you start to broaden, because there is always some segment of the organization that usually addresses some component that you are trying to encompass in compliance. You don't want to reinvent the wheel. What you want to do is pool those resources that are within your system and work together. Whether it is you doing the work or another department doing the work, it is all under the umbrella of what we call compliance. Compliance has been around in our business for a long time; it just has never been formalized into a program until now.

Troklus: Do you think that there is a direct correlation between adequate resources and commitment?

Vacca: Yes, I do. I think that the business priorities—keeping your bottom line at least budget neutral—and commitment are two things in my mind that interrelate. If you can't get the resources that you need to be able to run a program effectively, then the odds are that the commitment is lacking and your program is bound to fail.

Troklus: What would you consider as the top three pieces of information that your board members should know about the compliance program?

Vacca: I think your board members definitely need to know their responsibilities and accountability when it comes to compliance. It is absolutely critical for board members to be knowledgeable about what compliance is. Sometimes we develop parallel systems and people think compliance is just a "Medicare billing program." It is a challenge to help board members understand that compliance is in every aspect of their business and to help give them day-to-day examples. For instance, when they approve a new business venture, my challenge is to make sure that they understand that when they are going through the process of due diligence, they are ensuring compliance elements are met. Sometimes the board members view those as legal elements and don't correlate legal with "compliance." However, the two can go hand in hand and operational issues often accompany these aspects.

It is also important that board members understand the questions they need to ask. They need to know that they are protecting their community assets by ensuring that they are doing proper due diligence in their questions. I think board members don't need to micromanage, by any means, but they need to be able to say to the CEO, "Are there any regulations, laws, standards that we left out in our process of due diligence? Are we assured that there are no compliance aspects that have not been addressed?" Sometimes we go into contracts and business ventures without even realizing there are more questions to be asked. That is my challenge with the board.

Another area is to keep compliance a priority for the board and to help them continually integrate compliance into all they do in their board roles and responsibilities. I go annually to all the boards in our system. They see me coming and know, "Yeah, Sheryl and compliance are synonymous." They are also familiar with my message of emphasizing the board's role in compliance. But once I'm gone, it's absolutely critical that they understand—and incorporate what they understand—into their role as a board member. So my challenge is to continually keep that awareness out there, keep it in front of the board members, constantly give them tools where they can integrate their role into that accountability, and ensure that they have the knowledge to carry out this aspect of their role.

Troklus: What impact do you feel certification will have on the position of a compliance professional?

Vacca: Obviously, certification is not new to health care. All kinds of professions have certification. The value will be in how it is recognized in the industry. I think certification is the best step toward standardization of knowledge for the compliance officer profession. Unfortunately, because of varying levels of knowledge, resources available to the compliance officer, and the different sizes of institutions, sometimes your compliance officer is absolutely the wrong person for that organization. At least certification will help us to make sure that there is a baseline knowledge regardless of background. The most important challenge is to ensure that the industry and the people who are hiring and evaluating compliance officers are the people who also recognize that certification is the key to advancing our profession.

Troklus: Do you feel audits should be conducted before the billing process or after?

Vacca: I don't think there is a right answer. It needs to happen before billing and after the claim is submitted. It is very helpful if you can do auditing on a concurrent basis, because you can catch the problem before it gets submitted and becomes a real problem. I think it is important to audit postbilling, because you don't always know that you are catching all your errors. You are not assured that what you actually got paid was indeed what got submitted because of possible software edits and/or the fiscal intermediary. Sometimes that final audit might identify a single individual who made a change to the claim after all input was completed. This could have great significance, because you will never be aware of that if all you do is audit prebilling. Due to the human element, it is absolutely essential to do both audits before and after billing.

Troklus: What advice do you have for a new compliance officer?

Vacca: I think the most important thing for compliance officers is to learn the resources and the expertise in the field and to access them. They need to start with the federal sentencing guidelines as their framework for developing their program. But a new CO needs to learn not to reinvent the wheel. There are so many tools that are available now. The Health Care Compliance Association [HCCA] is a tremendous resource to a new compliance officer, in intellectual ability as far as networking, and also in the tools that are available. Take as many compliance courses as are available, so that you can increase your learning curve, pick up the lingo, learn the way to develop programs, and figure out what works versus what doesn't work. I think it is absolutely essential to attend HCCA's Academy of Healthcare Compliance because it provides you a good foundation on the seven federal sentencing elements of an effective compliance program. The academy will also provide you a very small group to network with and also resources that you can access immediately. New compliance officers need to be very clear on their role before they go forward. They should know how they fit into their organization and how much support and commitment they actually have from their senior management before they step out that door. Commitment is especially important. It is easy to say that you are committed, but operationally you need to be very clear on what your boundaries are before you walk into the lion's den, so to speak. You also need that senior manager—in my case the CEO—to be right there with you when you are developing that program and committing to the fact that "yes, this is what needs to be done." Your voice cannot be alone.

In addition, the new CO needs to read. There are reams of documents from the government that assist all compliance officers. You can't do this business without knowing what is in the literature, being familiar with the government's focus, being familiar with your whole business unit's focus, and where your potential and real problems might be. I highly recommend not to hang your shingle out until all your processes are in place. Even though it is very encouraging when you start to get people to talk to you, before you know it, the floodgates are open and you have no process for handling issues. You can become overwhelmed. At first when starting out as a CO, I think it is a common tendency to encourage issues to come forward *before* your processes are in place. The last thing I would say to a new compliance officer is to get a support system. You are in such a difficult position when you first begin. Your job is vague to you even though you tried to define it explicitly in that new job description you just wrote. It is vague to those with whom you are doing business and within organization. It is really tough to be in a spot where you are managing by influence. Your power is in how influential you can be with regard to what you will implement. From those perspectives, you really need to have somebody to bounce ideas off of, whether it is a role model, mentor, or even just someone who understands compliance and understands your difficult tasks of implementing your compliance program. It is helpful to have that support to keep your energy, euthusiasm, and passion intact for your role.

Interview 8

Odell Guyton
University of Pennsylvania

Odell Guyton is the corporate compliance officer for the University of Pennsylvania. Mr. Guyton has extensive experience in compliance development, litigation, investigations, research compliance and ethics.

Troklus: Tell me a little about your experience and background.

Guyton: I began my professional career as an attorney, working as a local prosecutor with the Philadelphia District Attorney's Office where I prosecuted violent criminals and served as deputy district attorney in Philadelphia for about eight years. Then I was in the United States Attorney's Office where, for eight years, I prosecuted savings and loan fraud as well as violent organized crime gangs. For about five years after that, I was in private practice and specialized in complex litigation and criminal defense as well as *qui tam* litigation. Now I am in the corporate compliance office at the University of Pennsylvania.

Troklus: You have such an interesting past. What brought you to the University of Pennsylvania as the corporate compliance officer?

Guyton: In my practice of law, we were involved with what we call preventive law, which included the installation of compliance programs into major health care institutions to help chief executives avoid trouble, particularly with the federal government. The University of Pennsylvania contacted me as they were starting up their corporate compliance office. They wanted me to utilize my skills here.

Troklus: Is the University of Pennsylvania a centralized or decentralized environment?

Guyton: We have a little of both. We have a centralized operational structure, but the responsibility centers (the schools and centers, etc., that compose the University of Pennsylvania) are decentralized.

Troklus: With your experience, what do you see as the major compliance issues for academic medical centers?

Guyton: Emerging as one of the major compliance issues is the whole concern related to conflict of interest, having a financial or commercial interest in your research or the product of your research. This issue is emerging mainly at the clinical trial levels and arises in the context of pharmaceutical companies and the financial arrangements between a principal investigator and these companies.

Troklus: What types of information should be shared each year during the annual compliance education?

Guyton: In terms of specialized education, such as a billing compliance where you are part of a corporate integrity agreement, that is governed principally by the language in the integrity agreements. But in terms of general compliance awareness, I think there are several things that should be included in the training. First, there should be a discussion about what types of policies and procedures exist in the institution, whether they are up to date, and whether there are consequences for noncompliance. That is where I would start. Another area would be what I call compliance awareness based on an environmental scan. What types of high-profile incidents are occurring right now that place the institution at risk and of which the employees should be made aware? These are the major components that must be involved in any compliance awareness program.

Troklus: I understand that some medical schools are now including compliance-related topics, such as coding and billing, in medical school curricula. What is your opinion regarding this?

Guyton: I think the more you do the better. As a matter of fact, one of the things that I would promote is for new physicians to understand the importance of these billing issues and how they came about. It is not just about the government taking a hard look at how physicians are billing, but the reason for the investigation and what the consequences of it are. If the physicians are more attuned to the causes of these problems, they can serve as gatekeepers in the future to ensure that their documentation supports their billing.

Troklus: Academic research has come under increasing scrutiny in recent months. Do you see this as a growing compliance concern?

Guyton: Yes. It is one area of concern, because the rules are changing and the government is trying to get a handle on where it needs to focus. Yes, I see it as a major compliance concern in terms of potential risk, but that doesn't mean that the research has been done fraudulently. This issue is also separate from concerns of scientific misconduct. We have to look at what the problem areas are in terms of the government's expectation of compliance.

Troklus: What do you see as the top research issues that are not receiving the attention they deserve in academic medical centers around the country?

Guyton: As I mentioned, I feel conflict of interest is one of the major areas. The area of informed consent is also important, dealing with how much the physician actually discloses to the human subject volunteer to obtain full consent. This is not just obtaining documentary evidence that says "consent," but fully informing the research subject of what is going on with the research and what the possible research risks are. Withholding information may prevent subjects from exercising an autonomous choice about participating in the study.

Troklus: Do the enforcement initiatives on federally funded research just focus on academic medical centers, or is the problem even bigger?

Guyton: Well, I think to call it a problem is a little bit premature, but some of the concern areas certainly extend beyond those of academic medical centers, with issues such as genetically modified food as well as compliance in the pharmaceutical industries. Certainly the scope of the problem

could be much larger. The government is just now defining what it perceives as compliance concerns. So we have to step back and see where the government regulation comes in, giving us some guidance as to what areas are gray and what areas are bright white problems.

Troklus: What types of penalties and sanctions can be enforced for noncompliant activity that is found in regard to clinical research?

Guyton: One of the things to keep in mind is that every institution within the scientific community has its own best practices and its own measure of compliance. In terms of research misconduct and related areas, the institution's policies and procedures must be followed to the letter and intent of those guidelines. In terms of the sanctions, the only appropriate sanction, if it's a gross violation, should be termination or some other heavy penalty. An institution has to look at the status of its own policy and procedures, and whether or not its own sanctions are being enforced, before that question can be properly answered.

Troklus: Do you see the corporate compliance officer taking responsibility for research compliance, or do you believe it should be a separate position and department?

Guyton: I'll have to answer that question this way: I think that corporate compliance is everyone's responsibility and that it's not just the compliance officer who is operationally responsible. Each person who is involved in the area has to be responsible for compliance on an individual basis. The role of corporate compliance is one of oversight and monitoring to make sure that people who have the operational responsibility are indeed enforcing that responsibility.

Troklus: Do you feel the compliance officer should sit on the IRB[1] committee? Please explain.

Guyton: I believe that it may not be the best solution because of the potential for conflict. Perhaps a compliance officer can sit on a neighboring IRB or on a sister institution IRB, but not on its own IRB. If it was a consortium of IRBs or a regional IRB, perhaps the compliance officer could sit on that.

Troklus: Since compliance is still evolving, where do you see compliance in five years?

Guyton: I see corporate compliance getting involved in a number of different industries, including that of the academic medical centers, particularly in the area of pharmaceutical research compliance. I also see compliance building up an ethical base. It's not enough to have people simply be compliant with rules, policies, and regulations. There must be a culture of compliance that fosters ethical behavior so that people get in the habit of doing the right thing in the right way before it becomes an issue.

Troklus: Do you have any words of wisdom for an individual contemplating compliance as a profession?

Guyton: I would only caution that compliance is an evolving field. You should look long and hard as to what the issues are going to be in the next five years before you jump into compliance this year. The issues will be emerging very quickly and, unless you are equipped to ride the wave of change and to begin to drive institutional cultural change throughout your organization, you should not get involved with compliance. Unless you have the support of top management, the true support of top management, you should not get involved with compliance.

---

[1]institutional review board

Interview 9

John Steiner
Cleveland Clinic Health System

Mr. Steiner has seen compliance from many angles. Once one of the American Hospital Association's legal counsel, he is currently the compliance officer for the Cleveland Clinic. John shares his unique perspective on the challenges compliance officers encounter while helping their organizations implement effective compliance programs.

Snell: What is your connection to health care compliance issues? What experience have you had that relates to health care compliance?

Steiner: I am the director of corporate compliance for an integrated delivery system, the Cleveland Clinic Health System. I have worked as a health care lawyer for twenty years and as a compliance officer for two years. Principally, I look at compliance from both a legal standpoint and a structural standpoint, and how to ensure that people are aware of and understand key legal principles for the benefit of the entire organization.

Snell: The position of compliance officer is often viewed as very challenging. Do you agree, and if so, why?

Steiner: I do agree. Through my experience in helping to craft the first model compliance program for hospitals when I was working as senior counsel for the American Hospital Association, I learned how compliance touches not just legal issues but operational, finance, and human resource issues as well. The position of compliance officer requires thorough knowledge of how our payment program and regulatory system became so complex. Understanding how the regulatory side of compliance works and ensuring that your organization is complying with the law make it a very demanding job.

Snell: Of the seven elements listed in the U.S. Sentencing Guidelines, discipline seems to be the most ill-defined and the least talked about. Why is discipline such a difficult topic?

Steiner: From the standpoint of the U.S. Sentencing Guidelines, discipline is a touchy or difficult subject because those guidelines are designed to build a compliance program that reduces the likelihood of criminal misconduct, which requires the corporation to look inwardly at its employees' behavior. Defining conduct that might lead to a criminal act is extremely difficult, and not a task that compliance officers or compliance committees address very frequently in a very realistic manner.

Snell: Despite the thousands of pages of regulations, we write countless internal policies, sometimes holding ourselves to a higher standard. These policies often become outdated or poorly distributed, and frequently employees cannot recite the key elements of a policy. What can we do to improve our systems and procedures regarding policies?

Steiner: One practical approach is to focus on delegable responsibilities by business line, department, or division and help those subunits of your organization in identifying key principles, which in turn require policies and procedures that address the higher risk compliance areas. Make sure they are given enough guidance, but require that they write their own procedures to address the identified risks. For example, when contractors write to providers and point out error rates and request additional documentation, the form letters strongly suggest that a provider adopt certain interventions. Have a system to track and respond to the contractors' additional development requests (ADRs). If that mechanism is in place, employees will understand the significance of an ADR. The corporation will position itself as more compliant for purposes of the contractors' reviews and also if it has to defend potential whistleblower suits or other investigations.

Snell: How often should the compliance committee give an update to the board? What information should they share with the board?

Steiner: It is probably routine to include a compliance report every quarter, which is usually when the audit committee meets. Many members of an audit committee, the chair, for example, and a few other members, frequently serve on both the executive committee and obviously the full board. I would recommend quarterly reports to the audit committee, maybe annually to the full board. The content will vary. If there is an active investigation, a status report should be given. Measurable outcomes, or benchmarks, that are linked to compliance measures should be reported to the audit committee on a regular basis.

Snell: What can the compliance committee do if they feel their institution is not taking compliance seriously enough or dedicating enough time and resources to it?

Steiner: The best approach is to explain to the organization, the senior executives, and the key members of the board of trustees the fundamental risk of failing to comply with the law. Emphasize the lessons learned in the past five years since health care fraud became a high priority and federal funding was made available to the Medicare program contractors and investigative agencies. In short, you have to describe the evolution of fraud enforcement and explain that a voluntary program will buy protection from having to live with a mandatory program. The other point to make is that compliance is a good mechanism, by way of committee structure and follow-up, for solving problems identified by employees from different disciplines across the organization as well as by the Medicare contractors.

Snell: Many people feel the anonymous reporting mechanism is vital to the success of a compliance program. Why is it so important? Why does it sometimes fail? How can we ensure it is effective?

Steiner: This component of compliance is a release valve for an employee who is intimidated about approaching a supervisor. If the integrity is maintained and there are no retaliatory actions, then the reliability of the information is usually very sound. That is a lesson learned from the defense industry. Whether the anonymous hotline or reporting line is truly effective is subjective. The outside agencies, such as the Office of Inspector General, are interested in measurable outcomes, such as the frequency of use, the content, and the results of a reporting line.

Snell: Do you have any tips for conducting education? I would be interested in your thoughts on any aspect, technical compliance issues such as coding or general compliance education for all staff including administrators, physicians, and the board.

Steiner: There are two fundamental approaches that work well. The first would be to rely on computer-based training with well-thought-through content and pretests and posttests of proficiency. The content can be developed internally or externally. That approach is particularly valuable as platforms for computer-based training on personal PCs are becoming more standard. The second option is an inservice session in a lecture style or a more informal Q&A style, depending on the audience that you hope to reach. Because compliance touches so many different areas within a complicated organization, you need subject matter experts to help you determine the content, the depth of knowledge you need to cover, and the frequency of training. On the precise issue of coding, without doubt, you need sound coders and reimbursement specialists who are knowledgeable about Medicare program principles. At a minimum, they should be continuously tested on both Part A and Part B of the Medicare program.

Snell: Many folks have implemented most of the elements of a compliance program. They have now moved into measuring the effectiveness of compliance programs. Why is there so much attention on the measurement of compliance program effectiveness? Do you have any ideas on how one can go about measuring effectiveness?

Steiner: The compliance literature—both the OIG[1] model program guidance as well as the guidance for other industries—emphasizes having an effective program in place before a problem is identified. People are linking it back to the seven major elements and trying to monitor their program by measuring repeatable actions, such as the frequency of education and training. Those activities that are driven by the seven major elements of an effective program are fairly self-explanatory. Beyond that, there is no tried and true formula for measuring effectiveness, although measuring certain repeated elements of a program becomes the most critical. The industry has learned what the government—particularly the Department of Justice—will look for in health care. They definitely will look for the existence of a compliance officer, the existence of an active committee, and sufficient resources for the office to do its work. They will look for evidence that there is some level of compliance structure built into day-to-day operations, for example, a well-understood and -implemented tracking process for ADRs. In analyzing the effectiveness of a compliance program, the Department of Justice also looks for refunds based on analyses of situations where the organization has concluded it was not entitled to the payment.

Snell: Many people feel that the enforcement community has gone too far. They feel that the regulations are too complicated and vague. Do you agree?

Steiner: The frustration stems from the sheer number of regulations and, in turn, the slightly different standards within the regulatory scheme that the organization needs to know about and monitor. These range from the potential criminal misconduct of violating a portion of the Medicare statute with "intent" to commit fraud to a standard that can lead to monetary

---

[1] OIG, Office of Inspector General

fines when the organization "knew or should have known" that it was not in compliance. Given the range of potentially noncompliant behavior, providing health care can be very difficult and often legally risky.

Snell: The government feels that the health care industry is making errors on black and white issues. They feel that, despite their efforts to get health care to spend time to get it right, we are still making mistakes that reflect a lack of effort. Is this a fair representation of the situation?

Steiner: I don't think that providers are continually making errors in situations that are "black and white." One only need look at the HIPAA[2] legislation involving the privacy issues and the complications from that single piece of legislation. Look backward from there, to the recurring problems that providers have in sorting out what a Medicare contractor means when they issue guidances or local medical review policies, which often can be inconsistent between a part A and a part B interpretation of the same type of medical service. There are many examples of that unintended conflict in the regulatory scheme. The state program, the federal program issuing the regulation, or the private payer's health plan, however, is naturally looking at the issue from the perspective of its office. Nonetheless, all regulations funnel into one central point and that is the health care provider.

Snell: Everybody is worried about Medicare billing. Some feel that the commercial payers are going to pursue fraud and abuse more aggressively in the future. Do you feel we should be concerned with the commercial payers? If so, why?

Steiner: The risk of a health care provider violating a federal payment requirement that is similar, if not identical, to that of the private payer is a very real probability. An example is currently in the courts in New York City involving a private insurer whose case is being prosecuted by the Department of Justice against a private practitioner. It's the first use of the criminal provisions of the Balanced Budget Act of 1997, Section 1847, which is the section that defines a federal health care offense. That is a

---

[2]Health Insurance Portability and Accountability Act.

high-water mark in terms of the issue at hand—health care fraud allegedly perpetrated by a provider against a private insurer.

Snell: Do you have any compliance web sites, listservs, or weekly e-mail magazines that you use on a regular basis?

Steiner: Yes. I receive several from professional trade associations representing hospital interests. I receive several from private law firms and private consulting firms and also have, as do many, server capacity for communications with other compliance officers.

Snell: We often run into problems that could result in a refund. What factors should one consider when determining how far back to go in an audit?

Steiner: Often the answer depends on a careful analysis of why a refund situation exists. The refund may relate to a major change with an outside vendor, in a computer system, or in the labor situation of the provider. Look for those types of sentinel events to assess how far back to look. By now, all health care providers should know the legal statutes of limitation that apply, including the False Claims Act, which can extend backward up to nine years. That benchmark should not be relied on entirely, however. Instead, a thorough analysis of the facts and events that led to the refund should be explored first.

Snell: Some people feel that the elections of 2000 could change the future of the enforcement effort. Could the election change the current enforcement climate? If so, how?

Steiner: My sense of the compliance environment is that it will not change significantly for three major reasons. (1) Most Medicare patients probably expect either political party to protect the Medicare trust funds from "fraud, waste, and abuse." (2) We have implemented so many programs within the last three to four years that have yet to reach their maturity level. To disband or cease compliance efforts leaves organizations in a weakened position. Starting a program and stopping it is much worse than not having one at all. (3) It is a complex system, both from a federal and a state law standpoint. A repeated pattern of noncompliance is something that needs constant attention. The compliance program and committee's structure is the best method for addressing that concern.

Snell: We have seen an emphasis on lab billing, pathology, and several other issues in the recent past. What new issues is the enforcement community focusing on now?

Steiner: From central HCFA,[3] there is an effort to work more closely with providers to reduce the "national error rate," which, in part, is gauged by a percentage of errors by specific service. In 1998, the acceptable error rate for most contractors was 35 percent. That dropped in 1999 to 25 percent. Now, in 2000, it's 5 percent. Strictly from the program integrity side, they have heightened their expected performance levels of providers. On the enforcement side, meaning the OIG and the Department of Justice, there is continued emphasis on the fundamentals of correct coding and compliance with Medicare billing principles, including coverage principles. There is an increasing discussion about risks posed to beneficiaries as well as other patients from managed care payment structures. Beyond that, the industry annually looks to the OIG Work Plan for continued guidance.

Snell: When do you feel the enforcement community will remove the bull's-eye from the forehead of health care and place it on the forehead of some other industry?

Steiner: I have asked that question in the past, and the general response has been that any sector of the country that represents a large percentage of the gross domestic product, and in turn where there is significant government regulation, is fair game. We have seen it in securities, environmental, defense, and health care. Some speculate the next renewed effort will be in natural resources.

Snell: Recently, a compliance officer filed a *qui tam* lawsuit. Does this surprise you? What reaction do you have to a compliance officer as a whistleblower?

---

[3] Health Care Financing Administration

Steiner: It is a complicated issue. The fact that a case was filed and apparently the government elected to intervene does not surprise me. I would have to know more about the specific circumstances and facts to talk intelligently about those types of scenarios.

Snell: What amazes you most about the compliance problems that health care has found itself in?

Steiner: I suppose it would be a general sense that the sheer number of laws and regulations that could and do apply to an organization is only better understood once the formal compliance program is running. That is a surprise principally for those internal to the organization who aren't fully dedicated, who have not, by way of their position description, taken on compliance as their full-time responsibility. Understanding how the laws and regulations apply and finding pockets where there is lack of awareness are probably the most striking aspects of this type of work.

Snell: If you could speak to every CEO in health care in the country, what words of wisdom would you have for them with regard to compliance?

Steiner: Compliance programs are similar in purpose to the old expression: "An ounce of prevention is worth a pound of cure." In order to strengthen your position in a health care fraud enforcement environment, you need a well-thought-out and -implemented compliance program, which will make it difficult for a whistleblower or prosecutor to prove the alleged wrongdoing. In short, the compliance program should anticipate the key aspects of each and every law, so that a complaining party or investigation will not find "reckless disregard" of the law or "deliberate ignorance" of the law and the other types of behaviors that have led to so many successful settlements and prosecutions. Also, for the most part, risks addressed by compliance programs are not insurable.

Interview 10

Michael C. Hemsley
Catholic Health East

Mr. Hemsley manages the compliance efforts for Catholic Health East and is also the second vice president elect for the Health Care Compliance Association. As a result of his extensive voluntary work within the health care compliance industry, Mr. Hemsley provides our readers with a big picture perspective, while his legal background and practical experience helps the reader understand complex compliance issues.

Snell: What is your connection to the health care compliance issues? What experience have you had that relates to health care compliance?

Hemsley: My connection and my introduction to compliance come from health care litigation. Litigation and the reactive side of dealing with problems when they arise are only the back end of compliance. The untapped resource, from the litigator's point of view, is the lessons that can be learned from the litigation, how best to position the organization to deal with the problem when it comes up and avoid litigation in the first place. Preventive law is the front end of health care compliance.

Snell: The position of compliance officer is often viewed as very challenging. Do you agree? If so, why?

Hemsley: I have learned in my tenure as a compliance officer that it is indeed a challenging position, more than I realized from my contact with compliance officers when I was in the private practice of law. It is a challenge on a number of levels. In an industry that is under heavy budgetary constraints, you don't generate income. The best you can do is help the organization keep the money it makes, protect the individuals, and protect the integrity of the organization. That doesn't show up well in a budget. Managers largely have not yet bought into compliance as a priority in their day-to-day operations. Your program competes against other budgetary considerations and is initially viewed as a necessary evil rather than a value-added program. Furthermore, the breadth, complexity, and multidisciplinary nature of compliance are such that there is a real challenge in trying to establish and maintain focus and priorities in moving a program forward while addressing identified compliance failures.

Snell: Of the seven elements listed in the U.S. Sentencing Guidelines, discipline seems to be the most ill-defined and least talked about. Why is discipline such a difficult topic?

Hemsley: It is a difficult topic in that it forces the organization to make some hard decisions. It involves HR,[1] unions, and arguably, vendors, as terminating a business relationship can be viewed as discipline. Discipline incorporates remedial action, which can be supportive of the employees to make sure they get it right the next time, and graduates up to the ultimate sanction of dismissal from employment and potentially legal action. Often organizations haven't thought through the implementation issues of discipline a great deal because it's an element of the reactive part of compliance, triggered only after you have identified a compliance failure, be it wrongful conduct or simply a failure to participate in the education process. In order to make it work, you have to think through the options, the graduated steps, and the processes that you need to have in place in advance of the need to use it; the constituencies and policies impacted by your disciplinary policies and practices.

Snell: Despite thousands of pages of regulations, we write countless internal policies, sometimes holding ourselves to a higher standard. These policies often become outdated or poorly distributed and frequently employees cannot recite key components of these policies. What can we do to improve our systems and procedures regarding policies?

---

[1] Human resources

Hemsley: In terms of the ultimate success of a compliance program, policies are the application of the fundamental business ethics of the organization to specific processes, issues, or situations. Education policies and programs should start with the business ethics, the mission, and the core values of the organization, which will provide employees with a moral compass if they don't have the applicable policy readily in hand. Assuming that your policies are consistent with that business ethic, your employees will have that compass to guide them and are likely to follow the spirit and goal of the policy if not its black-letter rule.

One of the problems in maintaining current policies is that so many people within an organization are involved in drafting, revising, and implementing policies. It becomes a laborious process that drags out over time, and when those involved need to focus on more imperative issues, the policy process falls through the gaps. We need to implement a discipline for periodic review of policies that forces us to take them off the shelf, look at them, and determine if they still apply to how we in fact operate. Do we operate consistently with the policy? Does the law require us to change that policy? We need to charge a very focused group within each business unit and department with the responsibility of periodically reviewing those policies and keeping the policies abreast of our operational practices and legal responsibilities.

Snell: How often should the compliance committee speak to the board, and what information should they share with the board?

Hemsley: Regardless of how you task that committee, the board, directly or through its compliance and audit or similar committee, should be briefed at least quarterly. Guidance for the scope of reporting comes in small part from judicial decisions and in its majority from the government's expectations and common sense. The In re: *Caremark International, Inc.* Derivative Litigation decision of the Delaware Chancellery Court, although not directly on point as it is a shareholder derivative action against the board of directors of a publicly created company, provides some useful guidance. The decision provides some judicial guidance on the analysis of the board's fiduciary duties relative to monitoring business operations compliance with law and to ensure that adequate corporate reporting and information systems exist and hence information the board needs to receive to so assure itself.

The OIG[2] Guidance Statements give little specific guidance on board reporting but make it clear that the board should receive regular reports on the progress of program implementation.

Common sense suggests that the board needs to receive reports on program developments, significant identified compliance failures, and the steps management has taken to evaluate and address the issue with the government and within the organization to reduce the risk of such failures in the future. The committee should report in sufficient frequency, depth, and breadth so the board can say—to itself and ultimately to a potential prosecutor, jury, or court—that it did make good faith efforts to apprise itself of the business operations and that management has in place monitoring activities to ensure compliance with applicable laws. The board has that oversight responsibility. To meet that responsibility, management must also report to the board on the results of audits or other reviews of compliance with substantive aspects of law regarding business operations and risks. They must provide sufficient information so the board is comfortable that management is appropriately responding to compliance failures.

The committee or the compliance officer also needs to educate the board on a regular basis so the board understands the issues and has a meaningful context in which to assess how well management is addressing those operational risks. Obviously, significant compliance failures identified within the organization need to be reported to the board with the appropriate attorney/client privileges attached to such reports as warranted.

Snell: What can a compliance committee do if they feel their institution is not taking compliance seriously enough or dedicating enough time and resources to it?

Hemsley: Whether the issue is a compliance failure or a "shell" program, those involved in compliance must be willing to take the necessary risks inherent in bringing hard news to management, and to the governance body, if they are to execute their compliance responsibilities in the best interests of the organization. To do that successfully, they have to martial the arguments in support of "doing the right thing . . . ," to show management and ultimately the board how taking compliance seriously, despite

---

[2]Office of Inspector General

contending budget demands, is enlightened self-interest and truly furthers the corporate purpose. Ultimately, it rests in the lap of the board. If the organization is not taking compliance seriously enough, the first step is to apprise senior management of that concern—particularly the highest ranking officer in the corporation with ultimate compliance responsibility—with prioritized recommendations on what needs to be done to meaningfully address the situation. Additional resources alone cannot cause effective compliance.

It's almost a game of brinkmanship for the organization. Bringing these issues to senior management and/or the board creates an opportunity for the organization to address those issues in an appropriate, well-documented fashion. The rationale for whatever decision is made can be reviewed in hindsight and hopefully deemed reasonable. However, this opportunity to enhance compliance efforts also creates risk for the organization. If it doesn't respond in a reasonable manner under all the circumstances, you have created even greater peril because the issue has been identified. A circle has been drawn around it for a future prosecutor. It is a tough issue. But if a compliance officer and committee are doing their job, that challenge needs to be met. If the program is a sham and management and the board will not respond in a positive fashion (recognizing contending needs), then resignation may be a necessary consideration.

Snell: Many people feel the anonymous reporting mechanism is vital to the success of a compliance program. Why is it so important? Why does it sometimes fail? How can we ensure that it's effective?

Hemsley: Organizations are composed of human beings with familiar faults, foibles, and insecurities. The fear that a price will be paid for disclosing errors is all too human a reaction. Those who are the subject of an accusation naturally react by lashing out, reacting adversely, whether the complaint is justified or not. Anonymity therefore is a selling point for such programs. It should be promoted. The same rationale goes for the mechanism itself. You have to give people a way to get their concern to you in a manner that is the least threatening to them. Otherwise, reports will rarely be made and employees will go outside the organization. The risk of *qui tam* suits remains undiminished and that does not serve the organization.

The keys to the compliance program include self-evaluation, self-education, and self-discipline. Why does it fail sometimes? Compliance is not yet ingrained into the culture of most health care organizations. It is not yet consistently promoted. I have seen survey results that suggest that even those who receive program orientation not infrequently report little program awareness. Until the program matures and its operation and effectiveness are publicly demonstrated, employees don't believe management is sincere and serious of motive and that the hotline or other reporting program truly works.

How can we ensure it is effective? (1) Promote the program and the hotline on a continuous basis; make people aware of it and of its successful use. (2) Make people aware that it is one of many vehicles they can utilize to communicate with management and the organization. (3) Complete the circuit: Make sure the people who call know that there is an outcome, that their issue was considered, that it was substantiated or otherwise explained. Callers want to know that some action was taken or that they misunderstood the issue and there was some explanation for their concerns. Feedback will provide greater credibility to the reporting mechanism and to the compliance program itself than almost any other thing you can do.

Snell: Do you have any tips for conducting compliance education? I'd be interested in your thoughts on any aspect of education: technical compliance issues such as coding, or general education for staff, administration, physicians, or the board.

Hemsley: You need to give whatever group you're educating—staff, administration, physicians, or the board—the reason why the education is important to them. The key is to make it relevant to them personally. Make it relevant to their job function or position. No matter how you deliver the education, you need to do that. Obviously, the next step is to make it as user friendly and painless as possible. The smaller the group and the more interactive and flexible the program, the more effective the education will be. Last, follow-up is part of education. Get back to them on quiz results. Give them an opportunity as they apply the education to ask further questions and get additional information.

Snell: Many people have implemented most of the elements of a compliance program. They have moved into measuring the effectiveness of compliance programs. Why is there so much attention on the measurement of compliance program effectiveness? How can one go about measuring effectiveness?

Hemsley: "Effectiveness" is such a goal because it is the touchstone of the federal sentencing guidelines. The sentencing guidelines identify seven elements that are necessary (but not necessarily sufficient) for an effective compliance program. Ultimately, effectiveness is determined at the time of a sentencing following conviction of a federal crime. Nobody wants to wait until sentencing to determine whether or not the program was deemed effective in minimizing a sanction level. Effectiveness is also preliminarily determined by prosecutors in deciding whether to prosecute, civilly or criminally, or whether or not there will be a corporate integrity agreement associated with a settlement.

Effectiveness is a troubling concept in the industry. Toward what end are we being effective? Is the compliance program effective if we are only avoiding criminal sanction, avoiding prosecution, or avoiding errors? If the program has high aspirational goals, aren't the measures of effectiveness broader than if the goal is avoidance of program sanction only?

How do we measure such effectiveness? We can start with a snapshot in time of all aspects of a compliance program applied to all aspects of operations, patient care, billing, and coding—measured against standards set forth by the government and by our peers in the industry. That picture of the corporate compliance program, both in terms of program process and compliance with substantive law measured by internal audit and monitoring, needs to be subsequently retaken to determine the degree of performance change and to evaluate the nature and significance of that change against the available benchmarking data. Additionally, you need to factor in changes in your business operations that may impact on these results.

Snell: Many feel that the enforcement community has gone too far. They feel that the regulations are too complicated and vague. Do you agree?

Hemsley: Many in the enforcement community would agree that the regulations are too complicated, but they are necessarily advocates of the government's position. The OIG recognizes the complexity of the regulatory scheme, but they too are bound by it and enforce it. Have they gone too far? That is a hard question to answer. There have been stretches in cases because it's a matter of advocacy when the prosecutors get involved, and often we know only the facts from what is reported in trade publications, and that is frequently incomplete. The pendulum is swinging back somewhat, though, toward a more balanced enforcement approach as all parties are trying to develop some consensus on what is an error and what is illegal activity. That moderation will likely get little visibility, as it will probably be more evident in prosecutorial discretion in the types of cases brought. The cases going to verdict will remain high profile and controversial. Enforcement projects such as the pneumonia upcoding and the 72-hour rule campaigns will persist as providing the best return of the enforcement investment of resources. The ultimate effort is to get regulations that are clear and more easily understood and applied. Once everybody understands the rules of the game, the perception that the enforcement community has gone too far will dissipate a little bit.

Snell: The government feels that the health care industry is making fundamental errors. They feel that, despite their best efforts to get health care to spend time to get it right, we are still making mistakes that reflect a lack of effort. Is this a fair representation of the situation?

Hemsley: In any industry as large and as diverse as health care, you are going to find providers who will not take the time to get it right and who are either making mistakes or intentionally engaged in gaming the system. But nobody can credibly say that the health care industry is not making significant efforts to get it right. The problem is the complexity of the issues and the regulations. Many of the people who must implement these regulations don't have the backgrounds to deal with this easily. A good deal of education is needed to keep employees up-to-date on regulations that are frequently changing and vary significantly in terms of applicability and interpretation. The effort has been there. Of course, the effort has increased significantly over the past several years as enforcement has been stepped up. That will continue even if enforcement dissipates a little bit because the industry is gradually recognizing that these efforts are the cost of doing business. The risk of noncompliance is present. The price of noncompliance is too great.

Snell: Everybody is worried about Medicare billing. Some feel that the commercial payers are going to pursue fraud and abuse more aggressively in the future. Do you feel that there should be some concern with the commercial payers? If so, why?

Hemsley: Sure. Just look at *Caremark*. Federal enforcement efforts sought to obtain a return of funds that were claimed to have been wrongfully paid. They were followed by Medicaid and ultimately the commercial payers asserted their own claims. If the third-party payers identify a situation in which the dollars are big enough to make it worthwhile to go after a provider for significant billing errors or fraudulent conduct, they will do so. Why would they not? There is money to be recouped. The theories can be more difficult because they are subject to state law and contracted provisions. But anytime you have a significant or pervasive compliance failure, you have to assume and calculate your potential loss to include commercial payers.

Snell: Do you use any compliance web sites, any listservs, *Compliance Weekly*, or e-mail on a regular basis?

Hemsley: I routinely check the government sites, particularly the OIG and IRS[3] sites. From the industry side, I look at the major trade association site,

---

[3]Internal Revenue Service

Healthcare Compliance Association, and a few other association sites. I generally avoid listservs and e-mails because of the volume, the lack of specificity, and the time required to deal with them all. There are 18 other compliance officers in my affiliated entities, and we have our own listserv, so we can consult among ourselves.

Snell: Some compliance officers emphasize ethics training in their compliance programs, while others ignore it altogether. Should ethics training be an important part of compliance efforts?

Hemsley: The focus of the government's concern with effective compliance programs is the reduction of improper payments under federal health care programs and compliance with Medicare rules of participation alone. But, in the long view, I believe the answer is, yes. If you can give your employees a sense of your organization's moral compass, whether they know a particular compliance policy or standard or not, they will have a sense of the right thing to do. If they don't know the right thing to do, they will know to inquire. They need to be confident that the organization wants them to learn and will respond positively to those efforts. Building the moral culture of your organization will make compliance a natural extension and tool of that business ethos rather than a process that is largely viewed as sanction driven and imposed on employees. Ethics-based compliance is not without risks as it does set the bar higher than government requirements; although the bar may be higher, the risks of higher organizational expectations than mere avoidance of government sanction are of relatively little practical concern as the government will focus its evaluation on the results of compliance program efforts, not motivation. In my view, compliance is better promoted, received, and more effectively engrained in an organization if it is viewed as part of the ethics of the organization.

Snell: Some find that their top administrators turn up their noses at ethics training. Why do you feel that some administrators take this perspective?

Hemsley: It is a reaction to the pressures and issues on top of their desks on a daily basis, economic and otherwise. It takes a moment or two of reflection to positively link business ethics with business operations. That attitude has to come down from the top of the organization on an ongoing basis. It's an organizational challenge to keep that linkage forefront in the minds of senior management, middle managers, and on down through the organization.

Snell: We often run into potential problems that could result in a refund. What factors should one consider when determining how far back to go in an audit?

Hemsley: It depends on the nature and extent of the problem that you have identified. If you look at a current process, for example, you find somebody has been miscoding, or there is a prevalence of miscoding, you have to consciously decide whether to look back, and if so, why. The government expects an organization to document its rationale for its decision on the scope of its review of that problem. If you have a reasonable explanation for the judgment you made, they would be hard-pressed to argue that you did not exercise due diligence in analyzing the issue even if the government later requires a further audit. Some of the features or factors you would consider are directly problem-related. For example, in a coding problem, is one coder involved or is it a number of coders? Is it just one code or are there multiple codes? Is the error consistent? How long has that coder been on board? Should you go back to the beginning of that coder's employment or as far back as the statute of limitations? You have to take very small steps as you unravel the string to determine the source of the problem. You continually narrow the focus of any retrospective review. Document the process and analysis justifying your decision on the scope of the review undertaken. You need to anticipate certain questions. What is the justification for not undertaking a retrospective review? Are the limits you place on any such review reasonable? These answers are fact-specific. Someone phrased it "the 20/20 rule." Would you be comfortable explaining to a national audience on the TV show *20/20* the rationale for the decision you made relative to the scope of your review and audit? If you're not comfortable making that explanation, then maybe you haven't looked at the issue hard enough and you need to pursue the issue further.

Snell: Some people feel that the elections of 2000 could change the outlook of the enforcement efforts in health care. Could the election change the current climate? If so, how?

Hemsley: The election can have some impact on DOJ[4] priorities generally, but I don't think it will significantly impact the enforcement environment. Fundamentally, there is too much money involved. Look at how much money the federal government has dedicated to enforcement efforts at HHS,[5] FBI,[6] and Justice, under HIPAA,[7] and subsequent legislation. The government expects a return on that investment. There is far too much money being recovered by the federal government and too many new enforcement personnel who will need to justify their existence to permit a significant shift in enforcement efforts. You might see some change in attitude, for example, in terms of the level of fines and penalties involved in settlements, but as a fundamental issue of enforcement policy, the election is not going to have a material effect.

Snell: We have seen an emphasis on lab billing, pathology, and several other issues in the recent past. What new issues is the enforcement community focusing on now?

Hemsley: One issue gaining a higher profile is patient care, particularly in the subacute care context. We have seen False Claims Act prosecutions over substandard care in nursing homes. Those cases are frequently tragic. Obviously, significant and pervasive patient care deficiencies would catch most people's attention. With the increasing demand for eldercare services and reductions in reimbursement there is a heightened concern that the quality of patient care will suffer. False Claims Act prosecutions in the quality of care arena are politically popular as well as an effective vehicle to weed out the weaker providers and those who exhibit a pattern of poor quality care and who don't undertake self-evaluations and appropriate corrective measures.

Another relatively new initiative is an expansion of the DRG[8] audit projects. We have seen single-issue enforcement actions involving, for example, pneumonia upcoding and lab unbundling. A new strategy is to look at multiple codes simultaneously within an organization, taking the

---

[4] Department of Justice
[5] Department of Health and Human Services
[6] Federal Bureau of Investigation
[7] Health Insurance Portability and Accountability Act
[8] Diagnostic Related Group

largest DRG codes by revenue and essentially doing a reverse billing optimization analysis. Using Medpar or other available statistical data, a comparison is made of your organization against its peers to identify which of those high-revenue DRGs vary significantly in volume from your "peer group," where your organization is an outliner. That analysis would be a precursor to audit and potentially claims for overbilling. By proceeding in that fashion, they would arguably compare like institutions in DRG utilization and then pursue your justification for variance. In that respect, you are going to see larger settlements because you have more codes and more dollars at play per institution than in the single-DRG programs.

Snell: When do you feel the enforcement community will remove the bull's-eye from the forehead of health care and place it on the forehead of some other industry?

Hemsley: I think the bull's-eye will be on health care for long time. It will fade a little bit. It will probably become largely a cost of doing business. It won't be as sexy as it is now because it won't be as novel. Probably the next time that the target changes will be the next time there is a significant government financial exposure as a result of an industry practice. Look at the history: the defense industry with government contracting and cost overruns, then the S&L[9] industry bailouts, leading to greater enforcement and compliance actions within that industry. We now have the focus on health care. I can't tell you what the next industry will be, but the trigger mechanism is significant, unexpected government bailouts of regulated industry or of consumers as a result of failed industry practices and/or significantly escalating government payments to such industry.

Snell: Recently, a compliance officer filed a *qui tam* lawsuit. Does this surprise you, and what reaction do you have to a compliance officer as a whistleblower?

Hemsley: It's a mixed reaction. I have heard arguments that the compliance officer should be precluded from being a whistleblower. How can an organization be forthright in identifying and addressing vulnerabilities and

---

[9]Savings and Loan

failures if there is the risk that the compliance officer will become a *qui tam* relater? Most compliance officers are, by orientation, committed to the organization and to helping it do it right rather than looking for a potential windfall by being a *qui tam* relater.

I expect the government to be reluctant to support compliance officers as *qui tam* relaters except in extraordinary circumstances. Compliance officers as relaters will fatally undermine the very compliance programs the government is urging on this industry. The other side of the coin is the quandary that faces a compliance officer if, for example, he or she identifies a significant violation of law, has advocated to the highest levels of the organization that corrective action be taken, and the organization chooses not to take that action. What recourse is there for the compliance officer? If the compliance officer remains in the organization, knowing that the organization hasn't taken or refuses to take action and continues in a practice that most people would agree is illegal, will the compliance officer be deemed to have complicity in that practice? The option to withdraw, leave the company, is a tough decision for people with other responsibilities. These concerns and a frustration level may lead him or her to go to the government to stop that practice. Should they be financially rewarded for something that has been brought to their attention as part of their job? That is a different issue. It is a difficult call. Hopefully, the vast majority of compliance officers are committed to persevere in a sometimes difficult effort within their organizations and that management understands their issues and risks and takes appropriate evaluative and remedial measures in such cases.

Snell: If you could speak to every health care CEO in the country, what would you tell them about compliance?

Hemsley: Compliance is enlightened self-interest. It is in the best interest of the organization, in terms of protecting its ability to conduct business in this highly regulated industry; in terms of its reputation with the government, with its industry partners, and with its consumers or patients. It is in the best interest of individual executives in protecting themselves from claims of criminal or civil misconduct and, given the regulatory scheme, protecting their ability to continue to practice within this industry. That is the dark side of it. That is the very practical side of it.

It is a practice that necessarily costs scarce dollars. It is a necessary investment to protect the assets of the organization, to keep the money it has legitimately earned. The ultimate risks of noncompliance are less remote than they may seem and far outstrip the cost of a compliance program. There are uncertainties in this process, but the effort is expected and worth the effort.

Interview 11

Rob Sevell
Foley & Lardner

Through his law practice Mr. Sevell has provided the health care community with significant assistance during very difficult times. When a health care institution is having trouble interpreting regulation, Mr. Sevell is called upon to sort out the issues. He is also called upon to help clean up problems for clients who have been singled out by the enforcement community. His real life experience is invaluable to his clients and to our readers.

Snell: What is your connection with the health care compliance issues? What experiences have you had that relate to health care compliance?

Sevell: I provide compliance counsel to hospitals, hospital systems, and medical groups. Working for Catholic health care providers has been a major focus of my practice. I have had experience developing compliance programs and dealing with compliance issues on an ongoing basis, such as false claims, Stark, fraud and abuse, and so forth.

Snell: I'm sure you have worked with a lot of compliance officers. A lot of people feel that that position is very difficult or challenging. Do you agree? If so, why?

Sevell: I definitely agree. One of the reasons that it is such a difficult position is that compliance officers have to deal with highly sensitive and usually complex issues that can have a negative impact, not only on individuals, but also on the financial position of the institution. Compounding all of this is what is often a general lack of resources to assist the compliance officer in doing his or her job.

Snell: Of the seven elements of the U.S. Sentencing Guidelines regarding compliance, discipline seems to be the most ill-defined and the least talked about. Why is discipline such a difficult topic?

Sevell: It is very difficult to sit in judgment of other people. I don't think anyone likes to dole out punishment, but that is often the role of the compliance officer. And just as compliance issues often fall into the gray areas, the proper resolution of those issues sometimes can be illusive. This poses additional problems for compliance officers in imposing appropriate discipline.

Snell: Despite thousands of pages of regulations, we write countless internal policies, sometimes holding ourselves to a higher standard. These policies often become outdated or poorly distributed and frequently employees cannot recite the key elements of these policies. What can we do to improve our systems and procedures with regard to policies?

Sevell: Policies need to be updated regularly and need to be distributed to the right people. Appropriate attention must be paid to education as well. Sometimes policies are too complex and suffer from an attempt to address every conceivable issue. The result is policies that can be overwhelming and hence not easily understood or addressed.

Snell: How often should the compliance committee speak to the board, and what information should they share with the board?

Sevell: Generally, quarterly reports to the board are sufficient for routine matters: to provide a big picture, to expose the board to ideas on education and training, and to inform the board of the resolution of compliance issues and developments. However, when an institution is looking at a very significant compliance issue, there needs to be more regular reporting to either the board or a board committee. If the issue is especially sensitive, as is often the case, attention needs to be paid to confidentiality and privilege protections. In that case, you may want to address those issues to a more limited group of the board.

Snell: What can a compliance committee do if it feels its institution is not taking compliance seriously enough or dedicating enough time and resources to compliance?

Sevell: That trend may reveal a poor initial commitment to compliance by the institution. The best course, in that case, is to work with a compliance officer and the board members who do support the compliance program to reinvigorate the commitment. Another option is to request the board to provide resources to meet specific needs.

Snell: Many feel that the anonymous reporting mechanism is vital to the success of a compliance program. Why is it so important, and why does it sometimes fail? How can we ensure that it is effective?

Sevell: Anonymous reporting mechanisms are of a significant but primarily psychological benefit. In my experience, they are not widely used. However, you should not underestimate the psychological impact because it definitely enhances an institution's general confidence level in the commitment to compliance.

Snell: Do you have any tips for conducting compliance education? I would be interested in your thoughts on any aspect of education, from technical issues such as coding to general education for staff, administrators, and the board.

Sevell: In general terms, the best education is interactive, providing real-life examples with, perhaps, some role-playing. I have seen some good videos used in that regard. You need to be careful not to talk over the head of the audience. In terms of the education of specific groups—for instance, doctors who are responsible for doing CPT[1] coding—you need to tailor education efforts as much as possible to the needs of your audience to achieve the desired result.

Snell: Many of our health care institutions have compliance programs in place. They have moved into measuring the effectiveness of compliance programs. Why is so much attention paid to the measurement of compliance programs and effectiveness? Do you have any ideas on how to go about measuring effectiveness?

---

[1]Current Procedure Technology

Sevell: Effectiveness is very important. In fact, the government has said that it is as important as having a compliance program in place. One of the best ways to measure effectiveness is to conduct a survey to see if the organization is more compliant—for example, whether fewer mistakes are being made—after compliance efforts have been made as compared to six months or one year prior. It is also very important, in terms of effectiveness, to resolve problems in a way that enhances confidence in the compliance program by encouraging employees to comply with compliance-related values in the future.

Snell: Many feel that the enforcement community has gone too far. They feel the regulations are too complicated and vague. Do you agree?

Sevell: In regard to those people who have made honest mistakes or who might even have been sloppy in terms of recordkeeping or billing, the government has perhaps been too harsh. There is also a belief that the government has not been pursuing vigorously enough those who have engaged in intentional criminal acts. One problem, which the government has acknowledged, is that there is a tendency to pursue the easiest targets rather than doing the heavy digging that is necessary to prosecute intentional wrongdoers.

Snell: The government feels that the health care industries are making errors related to black and white issues. They feel that, despite their best efforts to get health care's attention and to get health care to spend time to get it right, we are still making mistakes that reflect a lack of effort. Is this a fair representation of the situation?

Sevell: I believe that the health care industry is generally quite good about disclosing billing and other errors and making repayment where it's reasonably clear that an error has been made and a repayment ought to be made. I know that my clients, at least, are making very significant efforts to do the right thing. So I think the government's belief that there is a lack of effort is not correct.

Snell: Everybody is worried about Medicare billing mistakes. Some feel that commercial payers are going to pursue fraud and abuse more aggressively in the future. Do you feel that we should be concerned with the commercial payers, and if so, why?

Sevell: I agree that there is definitely need for concern to the extent that fraud on an insurance carrier is involved. The insurance laws of many states impose liability on providers to an extent similar to that imposed under the Medicare program. But when you are dealing with private insurers, you usually are not involved with the same level of detailed rules as you are with Medicare, and it is not always as clear when a particular billing practice is a problem.

Snell: Do you have any compliance web sites, listservs, or e-mail magazines that you use on a regular basis and would recommend to others?

Sevell: I work with a wide variety of them. The AHLA[2] has a good listserv to which I subscribe.

Snell: Some compliance officers are emphasizing ethics training in their compliance programs while others ignore it altogether. Should ethics training be an important part of compliance efforts?

Sevell: I do a lot of compliance work for Catholic health care providers. Most of them, in fact, were involved in compliance activities long before the government became involved. Compliance is intimately intertwined with fulfilling a religiously based mission and furthering values-based health care delivery systems. Ethical conduct is a core element of these values.

Snell: Many top administrators turn up their nose at ethics training, stating that it is too touchy-feely. Why do you feel they take this perspective?

Sevell: Some administrators are focused only on doing what is legally required and not on doing the right thing. This focus is much too narrow.

Snell: When potential problems could result in a refund, what factors should one consider when determining how far back to go in an audit?

Sevell: There are two main factors. One is the applicable statute of limitations, which depends on the nature of the charge underlying the refund.

---

[2]American Health Lawyers Association

Generally, in the absence of fraud or reckless conduct, the statutes of limitations are three to five years. A second factor is whether it is possible to identify a specific event or factor in the past that could cut off potential repayment liability. For instance, if it is possible to determine that a particular problem is attributable to a software glitch and you know the date that the software was repaired or new software was installed, that can legitimately be used to limit liability.

Snell: Some people feel that the elections of 2000 could change the future of the enforcement efforts. Could the election change the current enforcement climate? If so, how?

Sevell: I doubt it. Being against fraud and abuse today is like being in favor of motherhood and apple pie. Both parties have embraced the issue, and it has proven to be a real revenue generator for the government, representing hundreds of millions into the billions of dollars of revenues in a year or over several years. So I do not see future enforcement efforts as being significantly impacted by the election.

Snell: We have seen an emphasis in the past couple of years on lab billing, pathology, and several other issues. What new issues is the enforcement community looking at now?

Sevell: A second generation of DRG[3] upcoding reviews is going on right now in which the focus is on coding pairs, rather than simply individual DRGs. Another issue that is coming to the forefront at present is quality of care—especially in the long-term care industry—on both the federal and state enforcement bases. Another area that will probably catch quite a bit of attention in the near future is level of service coding by emergency room physicians.

Snell: When do you believe the enforcement community will remove the bull's-eye from the forehead of health care and place it on the forehead of some other industry?

Sevell: I don't think that is going to happen in the foreseeable future, even with all the strides that the government has made in reducing fraud and abuse. The government is convinced that there are still billions of dollars of money lost each year to health care fraud or to mistakes in billing practices.

Snell: Recently, an organization's compliance officer filed a *qui tam* lawsuit. Does this surprise you? What reaction do you have when a compliance officer turns whistleblower?

Sevell: It doesn't really surprise me, although I think it is very unfortunate. Serious thought ought to be given to providing protection to providers against compliance officers and other people in whom providers have placed trust, to prevent them from capitalizing financially on information they learn in that position of trust. There are some very good public policy arguments that self-examination and disclosure should be encouraged by providing protection for providers who, in good faith, hire and rely upon compliance officers to assist them in the compliance process.

Snell: What amazes you most about the compliance problems health care has found itself in?

---

[3]Diagnostic Related Group

Sevell: What has amazed me is not the problems that health care providers are experiencing, but how broadly and deeply so many health care providers have embraced compliance, allocating significant resources in an environment that is experiencing a relentless reduction in the bottom line.

Snell: If you could speak to every health care CEO in America, what would you tell them about compliance?

Sevell: I would tell them that it's not a passing fad; it's here to stay. In the long run it is much less costly to allocate the resources that are needed to ensure compliance than to skimp on those resources and run the risk of catastrophic compliance-related liability down the line.

Interview 12

Alan Yuspeh
HCA—The Healthcare Company

Mr. Yuspeh started his compliance career in the defense industry and is now the head of a complex compliance program for a large chain of hospitals. He also is a member of the Health Care Compliance Association board and a frequent speaker on compliance issues. Mr. Yuspeh shares his views and experiences on facilitating compliance programs in a large and geographically dispersed enterprise.

Snell: First of all, what is your connection to health care compliance issues, and what experience have you had in the past that relates to health care compliance?

Yuspeh: I serve as the corporate ethics and compliance officer for HCA—The Healthcare Company, which owns and operates about 200 hospitals and about 85 ambulatory surgery centers. My official title is Senior Vice President, Ethics, Compliance, and Corporate Responsibility. I have been performing these duties for about three years. My professional background includes the development of ethics and compliance programs, mostly with companies that were part of the defense industry. I worked with these companies, and a handful in other business fields, from 1987 to 1997.

Snell: The position of compliance officer is often viewed as very challenging. Do you agree? If so, why?

Yuspeh: It certainly is a challenging role, in part because you are dealing with so many different substantive areas of the law, so there is a great deal of variety in the material. Also, you are charged with articulating and trying to implement a culture within an organization, a culture that, at a minimum, anticipates that people will comply with the requirements of law and regulation. In our organization, it's also a culture that articulates a set of values and tries to ensure that people will do the right thing in all respects, even in areas that the law may not cover.

Snell: Of the seven compliance elements listed in the U.S. Sentencing Guidelines, discipline seems to be the most ill-defined and the least talked about. Why is discipline such a difficult topic?

Yuspeh: Discipline is difficult to talk about because it tends to be very case dependent. Most people would like some articulation of what discipline is appropriate for what type of misconduct. Talking generically about discipline is not always helpful. If someone does something improper or violates the standards of an organization, everyone agrees that there needs to be appropriate discipline, but each organization has to sort out for itself what will be appropriate in certain circumstances. Some activities require the severance of the individual from the organization, while a lesser form of punishment may be appropriate in other cases.

Snell: Despite the thousands of pages of regulations, health care organizations write countless internal policies, sometimes holding themselves to a higher standard. These policies often become outdated or are poorly distributed, and frequently employees cannot recite the key components of these policies. What can we do to improve our systems and procedures regarding policies?

Yuspeh: You have to have a sense of what you are trying to accomplish. We have issued policies in a number of areas of primary compliance risk because we wanted to articulate the procedures that make it possible for us to comply with relevant laws and regulations. Policies and procedures are necessary because, in general, the laws are not easily understood. People need some guidance on how to implement particular requirements of the law within the context of a particular organization. Telling people merely that they need to know all these regulations and comply with them is not very helpful. Once you clarify regulations through more clearly worded policies and procedures, you need people who are responsible for overseeing these guidelines, who can identify when changes are required or how they are working. We have designated "responsible executives" in each area of compliance risk. These are individuals who have extensive functional expertise and operating responsibilities related to that function. These individuals help to develop the policies, oversee their effectiveness, and make recommendations for change.

Snell: How often should the compliance committee or the compliance officers speak to the board, and what information should they share?

Yuspeh: Having a committee of the board that is responsible for these kinds of matters is very helpful. For example, HCA has an ethics and compliance committee of its board of directors. It meets at least quarterly. Typically at those meetings, we update the committee on new initiatives and on the results of our auditing and monitoring.

Snell: Some of our colleagues work for institutions that they feel are not taking compliance seriously enough. What can the compliance committee or compliance officer do to encourage their organization to take compliance more seriously?

Yuspeh: You need to have the enthusiastic support of operating management. The key is to have a chief executive or chief operations officer who understands the importance of compliance and the consequences that can occur if it is not given proper attention. The more members of operating management whom you can sell on the importance of compliance and on the consequences of being inattentive to it, the greater level of success you will have.

Snell: Is there something we can do to ensure the employees' trust and make them feel comfortable using an internal reporting mechanism which may permit anonymous calls?

Yuspeh: There are several things. One is to make sure that people are never retaliated against for reporting a concern. Try to guarantee the confidentiality of callers when that is at all possible. Another way is to make sure that matters are conscientiously investigated and that a fair resolution is reached. People who call should be informed of the outcomes of these situations.

Snell: With regard to education, do you have any tips for conducting compliance education, whether it be technical issues such as coding or general education for staff, administration, physicians, or the board?

Yuspeh: For education on our code of conduct, we use videotaped professionally acted vignettes that set up problems and then encourage discussion about how to resolve those problems most effectively. We are increasingly moving toward some Internet-based training, which is training for specific areas of expertise. With this new format, we are trying to use interactive problems. The more you involve people in solving problems, the more engaged they will be and the more they are likely to get out of the training.

Snell: Many, if not all, organizations have implemented the elements of an effective compliance program. They have moved beyond implementation into measuring effectiveness. Why is there so much attention about the measurement of compliance program effectiveness, and do you have any ideas on how one can go about measuring effectiveness?

Yuspeh: It is helpful to survey employees to obtain their sense about whether they are aware of standards and whether they would do what is expected of them. It is also helpful to employ normal internal auditing mechanisms, which would check on cost reports and other matters that are susceptible to such auditing. It is also helpful to use various kinds of real-time monitoring. For example, we are in the process of implementing a powerful data management software tool that will permit us to look at DRG[1] coding and compare that in each hospital with national averages. It is also a good practice to conduct compliance process reviews to ensure that prescribed compliance processes are being observed. Some mix of all of these approaches can offer a meaningful program for assessing how effective compliance efforts are.

Snell: Everyone is worried about Medicare billing. Some feel that the commercial payers are going to pursue fraud and abuse more aggressively in the future. Do you feel that we should be concerned with the commercial payers, and if so, why?

Yuspeh: I would not want to characterize or address the question of whether we should be "concerned with" commercial payers, but I do believe that commercial contract compliance is a part of compliance. Comprehensive ethics and compliance programs should ensure that the obligations of health care providers that are set forth in, for example, managed care contracts are being met.

Snell: Do you have any compliance websites, listservs, or e-mail magazines that you use on a regular basis?

Yuspeh: We use too many to enumerate. We probably have 20 subscriptions. We have our own website, www.hcahealthcare.com. We have placed on that website all of our policies and procedures and extensive other materials. We hope that individuals will continue to use that and will find it helpful.

---

[1]Diagnostic Related Group

Snell: Some compliance officers emphasize ethics and incorporate ethics training into their compliance programs while others ignore it altogether. Should ethics training be an important part of compliance efforts?

Yuspeh: If you can incorporate ethics into your compliance efforts, the effort is likely to be more successful. We have seen in a number of other industries that individuals who do the wrong thing often know that they are doing the wrong thing, but there is insufficient leadership or a weak overall ethical message about the commitment of the organization to ethics and compliance. In part, a values-based ethics effort establishes a much stronger leadership message that the organization is serious about violations. In addition, many decisions arise on a day-to-day basis that the law doesn't cover, and people want an articulation of values and ethical standards on these issues. Talking about values and expectations that are more generally ethical and less specifically legal compliance energizes people more and makes them see the subject as more high-minded. It is also a way to engage people who are not involved in Medicare billing or the topics that are the focus of legal and regulatory compliance.

Snell: Some of my colleagues have encountered top administrators who turn up their nose at ethics training, stating that it is too touchy-feely. Why do you think they are taking this perspective, and how can someone deal with an administrator who feels that way?

Yuspeh: It depends on what the ethics training is like. If your ethics training has a lot of general philosophy in it or is trying to teach people personal values, it will be of limited value and will tend to turn off lots of people, including managers. I prefer ethics training that identifies specific, realistic decisions faced by individuals in health care organizations that clearly have an ethical component to them. Focusing on those kinds of hypothetical scenarios starts people talking about the values of the organization and how to make those decisions. If those hypothetical cases are clear enough and represent day-to-day decisions, managers will find the training highly relevant.

In addition, that style of training may force organizations to deal more concretely with some difficult issues. For example, in a managed care organization, there are constantly issues about coverage. In the view of many beneficiaries, a lot of ethical issues underlie those concerns. The best way to deal with the tough issues is to talk about them a lot, to articulate your values and expectations, and to give people clear-cut examples. Show them how to resolve it. Managers certainly should not view that kind of training as too amorphous or touchy-feely.

Snell: We often run into potential problems that could result in a refund. What factors should one consider when determining how far back to go in an audit?

Yuspeh: The primary factor in deciding whether you go back at all is whether you find a systemic issue. For example, if you find a chargemaster error—which gives you some certainty that there has been misbilling for some period of time—then you have an obligation to go back and look into those things. Ideally, you would want to cover whatever period of time in which you thought the error had occurred.

Snell: What amazes you the most about the compliance problems health care has found itself in? How did health care get itself in this predicament?

Yuspeh: I'm not particularly amazed. Whenever you have a complex regulatory program, there will be gaps in implementation. These problems and the subsequent necessity for an investment of greater resources are really not very surprising.

Snell: If you could speak to every to health care CEO in America, what would you tell them about compliance?

Yuspeh: They have to be mindful that the success of these efforts is fundamentally about organizational culture. They need to adopt this as a personal concern and send a continuous leadership message that they are committed to an ethical work environment, that they are committed to strong legal and regulatory compliance, and that they regard it as an important part of their leadership to establish a culture that supports that throughout the organization.

Interview 13

Peter Grant
Davis Wright Tremaine

Mr. Grant has not only practiced health care law for many years, but he has been at the forefront of the explosion of the compliance industry. Peter has helped the Health Care Compliance Association develop conferences and significantly increase membership, and recently he co-chaired the largest HIPAA conference ever conducted. He has helped thousands of people through his regulatory conferences.

Snell: Is the health care compliance movement the biggest crisis in health care, or are there other problems facing health care that are more significant?

Grant: There are problems in health care that are much more important than the health care compliance movement. The fundamental issues of an aging population and increasing expenditures related to scientific developments—particularly in the genomic, biotechnology, and pharmaceutical sectors—suggest that costs are going to increase, at least in the short and mid-term. We are going to have more elderly people and much more complex and costly cures. I don't think that the health care system in the United States has done the math. There is no way that Medicare pencils out in the long term. Something will have to change. For example, we might need to go from defined benefit to defined contribution.

I think that the government's fraud and abuse enforcement efforts started because the government didn't want to have to pay as much, even though costs were increasing. Compliance is an important issue in the short term, but it's really a symptom of the fundamental conundrum of American health care.

Snell: Are there any compliance lessons that we can learn from other industries, such as defense or finance?

Grant: My impression is that the first big compliance explosion was in defense in the 1970s. Financial services followed, but not nearly as pyrotechnically. A difference, I think, is that the defense industry is a highly consolidated industry that could respond by forming a single, not-for-profit organization, which articulated fairly straightforward compliance plans. Health care is a far, far, far more complex, pluralistic industry with many different types of providers, payers, and clinical regimes. It's not conducive to the type of overarching, mutually agreed-upon fix that defense was.

Snell: Are you aware of any politicians currently working on simplifying the regulations?

Grant: I'm sure many politicians would claim to be pursuing deregulation. HIPAA[1] was supposed to be an effort to simplify the rules. I don't see it happening. American society is getting ever more complex, particularly in the new economy, with all the highly technical advancements and with so much development in the scientific and clinical fields. We are going to be a very advanced, complex, regulated society in the twenty-first century. I don't see it getting less regulated.

Snell: You have conducted several health care compliance conferences. What are the steps to ensure that attendees come away with a feeling that it was a worthy experience?

Grant: Two basic things have to be done. First, you have to go to the regulators, the people who are making the decisions. If you are lucky enough to get them involved in the discussion, then you create a liaison between the people in the field and the people inside the beltway, and it's mutually beneficial. That's fundamental. Second, you encourage the compliance officers themselves to talk about what they do. They are the ones

---

[1] Health Insurance Portability and Accountability Act

close to the ground who really understand what is happening. If you can do those two things, there is an immense amount of synergy.

Snell: You always go out of your way to get government involvement in the presentations. What do the attendees take away from government participation?

Grant: They get to know the most current view of the law and regulations, as well as where these people think the law and regulation are going to go. Perhaps much important than that, they get to know the personality of these people, which, to me, seems relevant.

Snell: There are many different points of view about the problems in health care compliance. Some feel health care is not paying attention to the details and the regulations. Others feel that the regulations are too complicated and vague. How do you feel about the issue?

Grant: I am an observer of many sectors of this complex industry, compliance being only one. I'm not sure that I have a full fix on it. I do not think that health care is failing to tend to the compliance issue. If anything, it's overtending to it. That is not to say that there are not bad apples out there, but the great majority of institutions and individuals engaged in health care finance and delivery in the United States are acting in good faith. Most of them are undertaking real compliance efforts.

Snell: Do you feel that it is possible to simplify the regulations, given that health care is so complicated?

Grant: Yes. Just the evolution of the payment methodologies in Medicare and Medicaid are amazingly complicated. The question is, do you simplify in the context of the existing structure of finance and delivery, or do you do it in conjunction with a program for national health insurance? Once you start mixing those issues, it becomes very political. Are you really simplifying things, or are you trying to provide coverage for the uninsured?

Snell: What do you think about compliance officers who turn their organization into the government for a compliance issue?

Grant: I find it troubling. I suppose that's just the training I have had as an attorney; I have an attorney/client obligation and responsibility. There might be extreme situations in which it would be appropriate, but I find it very troubling.

Snell: Given that compliance officers, administrators, and physicians are already acting as whistle-blowers, what can we do to stop the problems that are occurring despite the fact that a compliance program is in place?

Grant: Effective compliance programs assure the compliance officer adequate opportunity to express concerns to the board of directors and CEO. If these concerns are appropriately addressed, whistle-blowing shouldn't be necessary.

Snell: How long do you feel that health care fraud and abuse will continue to be a focus of the FBI,[2] DOJ,[3] and OIG[4]?

Grant: I expect that for the next three to five years they will remain significant issues. What happens after that? New areas of concern continue to arise, for example, privacy, data security, and HIPAA compliance.

---

[2]Federal Bureau of Investigation
[3]Department of Justice
[4]Office of Inspector General

Interview 14

Robert Dondero
PricewaterhouseCoopers, LLP

Mr. Dondero is one of the pioneers in the health care compliance industry. He began working on compliance-related issues five years ago and has served as an interim compliance officer for a major teaching institution. He and his colleagues have brought beneficial accounting principles into the field of compliance, which has helped immensely in turning compliance into a respected and effective profession.

Troklus: When did you first get involved in health care compliance?

Dondero: My initial exposure to health care compliance was probably about six or seven years ago, and it related to a self-disclosure matter with respect to both the Medicaid and the Medicare programs. One of the interesting things that I've seen regarding self-disclosures and even settlement agreements is the relatively low bar that was set up with respect to complying with provisions of that settlement agreement. That particular one focused mostly on education.

Troklus: How has compliance evolved since you started work in the field?

Dondero: I've seen some very meaningful evolution in a couple of areas. First, the management teams and the board are very much more involved than they have been in the past. I think the Health Care Compliance Association (HCAA) heightened awareness of outside board members' involvement with compliance activities, and how they focus their attention on management and the fact that the institution is attempting to do the right thing.

Also, six or seven years ago, there were many part-time compliance officers and individuals who served in a compliance officer role, who probably spent no more than two hours a month on compliance. The role has evolved into a full-time position, with both management and governance closely looking at it. The compliance officers are bringing a much more structured environment to health care institutions. I see that as very positive.

Finally, the individuals who are serving as compliance officers now are much more sophisticated about hospital operations, and they understand the "pressure points" for compliance matters within a particular organization.

Troklus: There is a tremendous amount of work in compliance. In what areas are health care organizations looking for outside help?

Dondero: Many institutions are now trying to determine whether their compliance programs are effective. Are the compliance initiatives, goals, and objectives approved by the board being met? Many institutions also are requesting monitoring and auditing assistance, particularly with regard to some of the more technical areas, whether it's a physician billing matter or a hospital billing matter. Last, there are still many requests for assistance with investigations, and for individuals to serve in an internal review organization (IRO) capacity.

Troklus: What measures are organizations taking to ensure that compliance programs are effective?

Dondero: I believe the management teams and the compliance officers are looking more closely at how the internal education processes are working. Do the employees understand and retain what is taught? Has the coding improved as a result of this education? The board is assessing the attitude of management, trying to get a sense that management has bought into the compliance program and the compliance practice to ensure that the organization is maintaining compliance with rules and regulations.

Troklus: Do you feel that health care administrations are becoming more concerned or less concerned about compliance? Are they becoming numb to the frequency of settlements?

Dondero: I don't believe they are becoming numb at all to the frequency of the settlements. HCFA[1] and all of the other regulatory bodies are going to maintain a vigilant watchdog view of the health care industry. As individual situations present major problems to the government and the health care industry, you will continue to see regulatory agencies assess whether those same facts and circumstances exist at a broader range of hospitals.

Troklus: Do you find that, in general, compliance officers have the control and authority they need to do their jobs effectively?

Dondero: In more and more cases, compliance officers are viewed as part of management. They have direct and ready access to certain members of the board, whether it is a compliance committee or an audit committee. On balance, yes, the compliance officers do have that control. In fact, that is all one of the important areas that any company should look at in determining whether an organization has an effective compliance program.

Troklus: Do you think that compliance budgets are adequate? Do you see a direct link between adequate compliance budgets and commitment?

Dondero: Generally, compliance budgets are adequate. We advise hospitals and compliance officers that regardless of the amount of money that they budget to a compliance department, make sure that it is prudently spent and that the compliance program is working effectively to meet its objectives. For example, if an institution is a little more concerned about monitoring and auditing, and the budget is limited, then the amount for that year should be focused toward monitoring and auditing. In linking the budgets and commitment, it is also important to ensure that the board is aware of how much has been budgeted for compliance activities, and to get the board's buy-in.

Troklus: Many people have trouble writing a request for proposals (RFP). What are the most important components of an RFP?

---

[1] Health Care Financing Administration

Dondero: Most importantly, the RFP should be clear about the form and content of the deliverables. There should be a very clearly defined explanation of what the provider or compliance officer would like to have as the final objective when that deliverable is presented to the compliance team or the board. One of the ways to ensure that you will have a well-thought-out compliance RFP is to be inclusive in your discussions with the hospital staff. For example, collaborate with other members on the compliance committee and get their viewpoints. Understand the risks that they see and the areas on which they would like to focus. Once everyone agrees on the scope of the project, present it to the appropriate board members and get their approval. If the project is clear to the board members in of terms scope, form, and content of deliverables, it will be clear to the companies from which the compliance officer is seeking assistance.

Troklus: What are the most important considerations for selecting an outside consultant?

Dondero: Experience is most important. The consultant and the firm should have experience from multiple occasions and in multiple complex situations. It is also important to assess the strength of the companies from which the compliance officers are seeking proposals. There should be a significant number of people available to provide the services being requested, and the company should have some staying power.

Troklus: What parts of a compliance program do you feel are the most difficult for health care organizations to implement?

Dondero: I have seen three areas that cause particular stress for compliance officers and providers. The first is doing large-scale education sessions. Coordinating hundreds and hundreds of people is a challenge in itself. The skill levels and educational levels vary within the large group of people that has to be trained. Ensuring that the training provides valuable insight to those employees is, and will continue to be, a challenge. A second challenge for compliance officers and their boards is determining how to measure whether their compliance program is operating effectively, not only from the standpoint of ensuring that the goals and objectives stated in the compliance program are being met, but that the compliance initiatives are cost-effective to the organization. The third area that I believe provides challenges and difficulties to institutions is auditing and monitoring, specifically with regard to technical billing and coding issues within the hospital and the physician operations.

Troklus: What trends do you see emerging in health care?

Dondero: One consistent trend that I see is a continued tension regarding financial challenges within the organizations. Managed care and the continued budget reductions (or at least flattening of the revenue stream) for many providers will continue to cause a financial challenge. That financial challenge will directly impact the amount of money that institutions are willing to spend on compliance; so again, compliance officers have to really focus on spending the money appropriately and wisely, and they must bring a lot of value to the institution for the amount that has been allocated to compliance efforts. The regulatory bodies will remain ever vigilant, and that will continue to cause stress within the management teams. They'll need to ensure that all of the bills and the operations of the institution are being handled appropriately, and at the same time manage the cost structure of the organization. Finally, I think the continued aggressive actions of *qui tam* relaters will be significant. I believe that is a trend that is going to continue in the near future and probably long after that as well.

Troklus: What should health care organizations consider when contemplating self-disclosure?

Dondero: Legal counsel, the board, and management clearly have to be on the same page, and they must have a very strong understanding of the particular situation. Generally, the details of circumstances coupled with legal advice will determine whether the self-disclosure item is of the type that really should be disclosed, or whether it is something that can be handled through a fiscal intermediary.

Troklus: What background is best suited for the compliance officer position?

Dondero: In today's world, I think the individual should possess very strong executive presence. He or she should not only be able to work effectively with senior management, but also be able to handle him- or herself in the boardroom and negotiate the way through some complex board situations. A compliance officer has got to be extraordinarily bright; must understand the business issues, the regulatory issues, the operational issues; and must be able to articulate those to the board and management. It has to be an individual who is comfortable with change, and who is confident enough in his or her own abilities to move an organization through change. Basically, the compliance officer should be a people person able to deal with very difficult situations in a positive, proactive, and professional manner.

Troklus: What information should the compliance officer present to the board?

Dondero: Most board members really appreciate an update on regulatory matters. They want to know what is happening throughout the country on a real-time basis, as well as where some of the regulatory bodies could be focusing their activities in the future. Another area that should be discussed on a regular basis is the work plan. At the beginning of the year, it's likely that the compliance officer will present a work program to the board that will entail a number of steps and procedures to be performed throughout the year. So, keeping the board current on the status of that work plan and what has been accomplished to date is very important. For example, hotline activity is a common theme in many update sessions, even more so if the institution is involved in a self-disclosure or other type of investigation. The board committee should be up to date on the activities regarding any type of investigation.

Troklus: How often should the compliance officer report to the board?

Dondero: Again, that depends on circumstances. In institutions that are first getting their compliance programs implemented, it isn't uncommon to have monthly updates with the board, especially if you have certain board members who are very proactive and very interested in seeing the institution's progress. As the compliance program and compliance process within the organization mature, usually the organization moves to quarterly or even semiannual updates.

Troklus: How can you encourage physician support and involvement?

Dondero: One very effective method is looking to the physician ranks, to a respected physician within the group. It doesn't necessarily have to be the chief medical officer, although I have seen that work effectively at some academic medical centers. What is important is to find the physician who is interested and proactive in compliance; he or she would have a good understanding of what compliance means to the institution, what compliance means to their individual practices, and what the benefit will be to the patients. Once that respected physician is identified, ensure that he or she has adequate time to spend on compliance matters, because that is also very important.

Troklus: How do you see compliance evolving in the next five years?

Dondero: I think it will continue to transition to a much more formal system along the lines of what financial institutions have had in operation for a number of years. Banks have had compliance departments ingrained into their control structures for years and years, and their compliance officers work closely with senior management, the board, internal auditors, and others within financial and banking institutions. I think we'll see the health care compliance officer role meld into that same type of atmosphere. Also, we have seen over the past couple of years that compliance officers and their departments are beginning to have a much more trusting relationship with other departments and employees in the hospital. The compliance department won't be viewed as "big brother," but as an integral part of the provider's business that provides solutions to the hospital and ensures that the policies and procedures of that hospital are followed on a regular, consistent basis.

Troklus: Do you have any advice for new compliance officers?

Dondero: Be very careful not to overreact or attack a situation until you are comfortable that you have all the facts. It's not unusual for inexperienced compliance officers to do that, and sometimes they lose the respect of senior management and the board. The flip side of that is that you don't want to underreact either, because you will also lose their respect. Do all of the appropriate due diligence and fact finding, bring in all the appropriate people who are central to the matter, and ensure that you have all the facts and that you discuss them with the appropriate people at the appropriate levels. Whether you are a first-time compliance officer or replacing another compliance officer who moved on to another role, it is very important to understand the corporate culture of the organization and to get a strong understanding of why that organization is in its current state. Spend time discussing matters and corporate culture and identity issues with senior management, the board members, and the various department heads as well. Understand how compliance was viewed prior to the new compliance officer's arrival. Doing appropriate due diligence, as I will call it, taking the temperature of the organization, and spending the right amount of time understanding the fact patterns are all very beneficial.

Interview 15

Eugene Porter
Montefiore Medical Center

Eugene Porter is vice president of audit services and corporate compliance officer for Montefiore Medical Center. Mr. Porter brings extensive experience in the area of auditing/monitoring and has developed a unique system at Montefiore.

Troklus: To set the stage, tell me about your organization.

Porter: Montefiore Medical Center (MMC) is a not-for-profit, acute care teaching hospital in the Bronx, located in New York City. MMC is the university hospital primary affiliate for the Albert Einstein College of Medicine. The Medical Center has 1,060 certified beds in two facilities in the Bronx: the 679-bed Henry & Lucy Moses Hospital and the 381-bed facility at the Jack D. Weiler Hospital of the Albert Einstein College of Medicine. MMC also operates an 80-bed skilled nursing facility, and we are one of the largest hospital-based home health agencies in the country. The Medical Center has two methadone maintenance treatment programs. Montefiore is New York State's largest sponsored renal dialysis program and has 27 primary care network sites located in the Bronx, Westchester, and Manhattan. Contract Management Organization/Integrated Physician Association (CMO/IPA) has 2,000 physicians with contracts for full-risk capitation covering 43,000 lives and partial-risk capitation agreements covering 45,000 members.

We just established an affiliation with HIP and assumed the care of 110,000 of their enrollees in the Bronx and Westchester. MMC's new jewel is the Children's Hospital, which was designed with Carl Sagan's input.

Troklus: What does the structure of the compliance program look like?

Porter: From its inception, the compliance program has received strong board of trustee support. The board of trustees approved a compliance charter, which establishes, defines, and authorizes the compliance program and officer. The compliance officer has a dual reporting to the compliance subcommittee of the board of trustees and to the president of the Medical Center. There is also an executive compliance committee that provides guidance and support to the compliance program. The executive compliance committee is composed of the president of the Medical Center, all MMC executive vice presidents, and senior vice presidents from various disciplines (i.e., clinical, development, finance, HR, legal). All areas of the Medical Center are represented on the executive compliance committee. We also have functional compliance departments, where we delegate the corporate compliance to the department level. They correspond to the areas that the OIG[1] has developed compliance guidelines (laboratory, home health, radiology and Montefiore Medical Group). The functional compliance departments are authorized and come under the umbrella of the Corporate Compliance Office.

Troklus: Was there a certain incident that caused your company to implement a compliance program?

Porter: Not really. Before the OIG finalized its regulations, MMC already had what could be considered a compliance program. Montefiore's motto has always been "doing the right thing is the right thing to do." In 1968, our board of trustees directed that MMC have a policy for checking for billing compliance, so we set up committees for that purpose. When it came time to set up a compliance program, MMC already had structures in place. The development of a corporate compliance program was something the institution felt we needed to do and not just what we were asked to do.

Troklus: What position did you hold prior to becoming the compliance officer?

---

[1] Office of Inspector General

Porter: I was the vice president of the Department of Audit Services. I was asked to develop, implement, and administer MMC's corporate compliance program. I am now the vice president, Department of Audit Services, and corporate compliance officer.

Troklus: What background do you feel is essential for a compliance officer to have?

Porter: I think that it should be someone who has knowledge of regulations and has worked with people at all levels of the organization, so they already have a built-in network and established relationships. That person must be able to bring together the different areas of their health care institution and help with problem solving. The compliance officer should have the confidence of the board and the executive staff. The person should be a senior position and report to the most senior executive in the institution and have a line of independent reporting to the board. The right person should already have been looked upon as a facilitator.

Troklus: I understand that you have an audit program to be proud of. Would you like to tell me a little about your audit program?

Porter: Yes, we are proud of it. We perform process audits. When it came to the area of compliance, we had the choice of having the Department of Audit Services conduct compliance audits or having a separate compliance group do compliance audits. Fortunately, I have a staff that is clinically oriented and process-based. For example, I have an RN who previously was an assistant VP of quality management service. There is an RN on the staff who previously was an administrator for quality control and medical records. Another staff member has a CPA, an RN, an MBA and worked in health care. We have a director of computer audit and analysis techniques position who works with seven major MMC systems and the application systems to perform analysis, benchmarking, and trending. Finally, we have a compliance director who has had extensive experience in administering municipal and regulatory agencies. All staff go though both IDC-9 and CPT intermediate coding training. We have always had auditors with multiple skills. The capabilities of the audit staff allowed us to get involved in compliance very easily.

We wanted to improve the synergy between compliance and audit. By combining facets of these two tasks, we enhance effectiveness, improve productivity, eliminate redundancy, and provide for a more efficient use of our resources. We merged reporting systems, staff, and communications. This improvement enhances response time to critical issues. We are able to perform a risk matrix that includes the compliance elements that are factored into the selection of audit candidates. The department of audit services also does self-assessments for compliance at the beginning of every audit as a control measurement. Often, a compliance issue will prompt us to perform a risk matrix, which may trigger a full-scale audit. We may find billing problems during an audit, and we can send our compliance billing experts who perform reviews, identify issues, educate staff, and perform ongoing monitoring of an area. This system works because we have staff who are multidisciplined and who are able to look at the entire institution from both compliance and clinical vantage points.

Also, we make a distinction between auditing and monitoring. We have a separate billing compliance monitoring group that is fully trained in billing and coding. They go into a physician's office, for example, and pull a sampling of charts; they review them to see how much training is needed for the billers, the physicians, or maybe both. That is what we consider monitoring. We like to use compliance billers as a resource when people call us and say, "We need help. Can we have training? Can we have advice?" We separated this service from auditing. The traditional auditing is done by the Department of Audit Services. The two groups are very distinct but are totally collaborative and synergistic.

Troklus: What time frame do you feel should be set for conducting audits (e.g., monthly, quarterly, annually)?

Porter: I don't know that we set specific time frames. Within the health care industry, audit has to be flexible and very responsive. Auditing and monitoring are ongoing activities. You may look at different areas within different periods of time, but I don't think there is ever a time you would not visit an area periodically.

Troklus: Do you feel it is best to have internal staff conducting the routine audits, or should they be done by an external firm?

Porter: It depends on the expertise and skill levels that you have within the audit department and within your organization. If you don't have the disciplines that you need to do the job right internally, you should definitely go external. In any institution that has an internal function with diversity and depth of skills, it is always better to do it in-house. However, I recommend very strongly that it be done in-house if at all possible because you know the people, you know the areas, you know how they relate, you know where some of the potential breakdowns may be. You have people who will talk to you more intimately about the issues. Corporate culture is very important in compliance programs. I think that all compliance departments should work to integrate their programs into the corporate culture of the organization. For an external audit program to do that would be very hard. If it is your goal to integrate compliance into corporate culture, I can only see it being done internally.

Troklus: We talked about a billing audit. Are there certain pieces of information that should be gathered prior to beginning that audit?

Porter: We do billing audits and billing monitoring, but they both need the same kind of information. Before the audit, you want to know the automated systems and the billing systems. You must have access to the charts. Someone knowledgeable about the billing systems must be identified to assist the auditor. Every part of the billing process between the time a patient is seen and the time that the bill goes out the door has to be totally accessible to the auditor. A flowchart of the whole billing activity should be one of the first things you ask for.

Troklus: Does your facility use a particular audit tool to conduct your billing audits? Do you use any published audit tool?

Porter: When we do automated auditing, we use many applications for analysis, trending, and risk assessment. We use various applications and to bring the data from various databases together in one file. In order to do an analysis or trending, we must be able to go between different databases. Our automated software tools allow us to bring in any database and to perform comparisons, which we do on an regular basis. We also use report writers that are specific to the individual billing systems.

Troklus: You read a lot about having an external audit of the audit process done. How often do you feel that this is really necessary, or do you feel it is necessary at all?

Porter: The external auditors and internal auditors must work together. When we do our audit schedule, we have input from the external auditors, and when they are doing the year-end audit, they get input from us. If you are working together regularly, then I don't think it is as important to have an external audit of the internal process. If you do not have that relationship with your external auditors, you should sit down together at least once a year and then whenever any major changes happen within the organization or within the structure of the audit function. We also use some of the same automated tools as our external auditors so we are able to exchange information.

Troklus: Do your auditing and monitoring result in feedback to the physicians as well as in helping you to develop new educational initiatives?

Porter: Oh, absolutely. And that goes back to where we make that split between monitoring and auditing. The monitoring group uses the tests or the review, as opposed to audit, to identify areas where training is needed. For example, when compliance billing does its initial review, they will determine whether it is a department problem and, if it is, they will then do a training of the department. Then they will come back maybe 60 days later and take another number of records and go over them to see if the training solved the problem. If the problem continues, the solution may be to train just a few physicians or just a few of the billers. Billing compliance uses information from the monitoring process to identify what kind of training or reinforcement of training is needed. An audit is used for an overall direction. For example, if we see that there is a process breakdown, that would come out more in the audit. The reviews of the billing area are done to monitor the effectiveness of our training program and to identify opportunities for enhancement of that program.

Troklus: What kind of compliance education do you have set up?

Porter: Our corporate compliance utilizes a two-tiered educational process. All of our 13,000 employees initially went through the general corporate compliance program, as does every new employee. Then we have specific training (e.g., for labs, radiology, billing) for staff members working in those areas. Corporate compliance training is part of our mandatory annual in-service training sessions. Also, we participate in departmental grand rounds for physicians. We have interactive software training programs that we use for physicians and the billing staff, and we electronically track this education on line.

Troklus: Do you feel that a compliance program needs sanctions for noncompliance in order to be effective?

Porter: I would say that most of the people in our industry are conscientious and want to do the the right thing, because it is the right thing to do. Unfortunately, you do at times need those sanctions, however, as one more tool to help enforce compliance.

Troklus: What types of sanctions do you recommend?

Porter: The sanctions should be graduated and should depend on the infraction. The options could include training or retraining, a write-up in the employee's performance review, probation, termination, and even a report to the authorities and possible prosecution and arrest. You have to have a response for something simple as a misunderstanding or a need for retraining as well as for noncompliance that requires prosecution and incarceration.

Troklus: There is a lot of discussion on what the audit process should look like. Would you recommend for billing retrospective or concurrent audits, and why?

Porter: The only time that I would recommend a retrospective audit is if you have a systemic problem that could be fraudulent. Audits should be concurrent whenever possible.

Troklus: Is there a magical number of encounters that need to be reviewed for each physician? If not, how would you go about deciding how many to use in the audit?

Porter: A lot of it has to do with having a good risk matrix methodology. For example, initially for compliance reviews, we send out a control self-assessment questionnaire. We review the staff responses and compare those responses to the actual that should be taking place. We use this information to decide how many encounters need to be reviewed. The minimum would be around ten for a physician, but it would depend on the size of the area and whether there are any previously known billing problems for the specialty under review. I would definitely increase the number of encounters in problem areas to create a statistical sampling that would be more valid.

Troklus: The audit process is critical to the effectiveness of the compliance program. Do you see a further expansion of what constitutes an audit? If so, what types of things will be changed or added?

Porter: Compliance is not just billing, although that is what has gotten the headlines and what has gotten the highest payback. For us, compliance and audit already overlap. When audit performs a review of an area, we use our compliance questionnaire as part of our audit program. We are also looking at HCFA[2]-identified problem areas.

Troklus: You seem so decentralized because you have several institutions within your system. Do you have compliance liaisons in those different areas?

Porter: Yes, we do. We feel the ultimate goal of any compliance program is to make sure that it is integrated into the fabric of the institution. We found that the best way to do that is to get to the core level of the institution through liaisons. Liaisons disseminate information for regulatory alerts; they help coordinate training, follow up on corrective activities identified by billing compliance and/or audit services, and give information for monitoring follow-up activities. Liaisons also inform us when there is a problem, and they do ongoing surveys to see whether or not there have been cultural changes or attitude changes. The liaison activities become part of their regular activity, and hopefully, because of that, become part of the corporate culture.

Troklus: What advice would you have for a new compliance officer?

---

[2] Health Care Financing Administration

Porter: Think about it very carefully and don't underestimate the importance or the demands that are going to be put on you. Before you start, get a total commitment from your board and senior management. Get a formal board resolution for establishing the compliance officer and function. This formalized resolution is extremely important to obtain before you start. The commitment that you get from the board and executives should include financial support as well as human resource support. You should also have a vision statement and an implementation strategy; don't just jump in. Finally, look upon compliance as a program and not a project. Integrate compliance so completely and seamlessly into the fabric of the culture of the institution and the daily activities of your associates that compliance is not a function or department, but a way of doing life. The individual should have stamina, perseverance, and a lot of luck! Finally, accept the position knowing that your compliance program will forever change the culture of your institution, if successfully implemented ("That's immortality?").

Interview 16

Albert Bothe, Jr.
University of Chicago

Albert Bothe Jr., MD, is professor of clinical surgery for the University of Chicago and executive director of the University of Chicago's Practice Plan. He is involved in the compliance program at the university and brings the physician's view on compliance.

Troklus: So many academic medical center structures are so complex. What is the University of Chicago's structure like? Is it centralized or decentralized?

Bothe: It's a hybrid. There is a centralized compliance office with a chief compliance officer and a small staff. In each of the major entities that form our enterprise, there is a compliance officer and often a compliance committee. That compliance officer will meet with his or her colleagues who have the same title on a regular basis, and with the chief compliance officer for the entire organization on a monthly basis. This ensures uniform policies, similar interpretations of questions, coordination of resources, and coordination of communication, which often spans more than one entity at a time.

Troklus: What is your role regarding compliance at the University of Chicago?

Bothe: I am serving as the compliance officer within the medical school, which is the employer of the faculty physicians. There is a symmetrical arrangement with a compliance officer on the hospital side, on the home health side, in the affiliated hospitals, etc.

Troklus: I know that many physicians run the other way when asked to serve on a compliance committee. What inspired you to take such an active role in compliance?

Bothe: As I arrived at the University of Chicago several years ago, this structure was just being developed. The leadership at the physician level seemed to be a natural responsibility for someone in the faculty practice plan within the medical school. It became an extension of the support functions for which I am responsible, and it helps the faculty do their job in a better, more efficient way.

Troklus: When we say the words, "in search of compliance," what comes to mind?

Bothe: It is a question of how to make compliance part of an organization's culture. At an individual level, it is how to make compliance part of the everyday awareness of people within the different components of the organization.

Troklus: Compliance is such a big issue for all segments of the health care industry. What do you see as the major compliance issues for academic medical centers?

Bothe: It depends on which part of the medical center you consider. On the physician side, coding accuracy is an issue, along with the constant education that will be required to understand the nuances of coding. Another issue is coordinating the multiple moving parts that go into the complete billing cycle. Finally, a major issue is compliance in the clinical research arena.

Troklus: So often I hear people say, "I have developed certain policies, but I can't share them with you." Do you encourage the sharing of information and networking with other academic medical centers or other compliance officers?

Bothe: Learning from peers is one of the things we don't do as well as we should in medicine. One of the potential barriers is that one institution's policies and procedures may not be applicable to another institution. However, I think of the analogy with the JCAHO[1] requirements, in which we are all working from the same framework. The actual policies and procedures reflect the individual characteristics of each institution. It is similar to the notion of "mass customization": same skeleton, different details.

Troklus: What do you feel the role of the physician is regarding compliance?

Bothe: The answer to that will depend on the level of physician to which you refer. At an individual encounter level, the physician is responsible for the accuracy of billing for his or her own procedures, as well as an awareness of the regulations. When a physician has leadership responsibility, not only must he or she have a certain content knowledge, but he or she must help set the tone that compliance is part of the principled goals of the organization.

Troklus: Do you feel physicians should be involved on the compliance oversight committee?

Bothe: It depends on their level of responsibility within the enterprise and how much their areas of responsibility touch the operational aspects of compliance. Certainly, the physician perspective needs to be represented in the education and the feedback loop that involves physicians. Perhaps, physicians need not be so involved with organizational information systems, budget allocations, or coordination within the enterprise. These could be left to others with managerial responsibility for those interfaces.

Troklus: Judging the climate today, what would you say that most physicians think about having compliance programs? Are they glad to have them in place, or do they perceive them negatively?

Bothe: The adoption of compliance programs represents a change in most institutions, and there is a distribution curve of how readily people adapt to change and make it part of their daily existence. We've had examples of the early enthusiastic participants. We've had many examples of reasonable adapters who want the situation clearly explained but accept it as part

---

[1]Joint Commission on Accreditation of Healthcare Organizations.

of doing the right thing. As with any change, there will be some resisters. The obligation is to move along the whole organization, recognizing that there is individual variation among physicians.

Troklus: What advice would you give a compliance officer in gaining buy-in from physicians?

Bothe: I am inclined to apply the change management models from organizational psychology. There is a significant change over the past few years in the level of attention compliance receives. One of the fundamental components is to establish the reason or the need for change. That means identifying both the internal and external factors. You need to be sure that you have public, explicit, unambiguous support at the highest levels of the organization. You need to communicate again, and again, and again, so that physicians can touch and feel what the compliance program means to them. They need to interact with it so that they can see there is reasonable feedback and that the system works in a manner that is perceived to be fair and has a high level of content credibility.

Troklus: In your opinion, should Medicare's Final Rule for Teaching Physicians be used by all payers, or should it be used only for Medicare?

Bothe: I tend to support the idea of having a single documentation standard across the entire institution because of the feasibility of implementing it, monitoring it, and enforcing it. It is more difficult to have different sets of rules for the same activities. There are also some important beneficial aspects about the teaching physician rules. Although at the outset they may seem onerous, they may actually improve patient care. That being said, there might be some unique areas that warrant further exploration. One example is the application in behavioral health, since the rules in various states and among various payers are different from most other E&M (evaluation/management) categories of service.

Troklus: Given the recent enhancements to the self-disclosure protocol, do you think compliance officers will be more likely to consider using self-disclosure?

Bothe: They are more likely to consider it, especially since it was promulgated as having lesser penalties. I don't know if it will actually be used more often. It needs to be considered on a case-by-case basis with in-house and outside counsel. You might get information either directly or indirectly from the carrier and make assessments about materiality because there are still some gray areas.

Troklus: What do you feel constitutes an effective reporting system?

Bothe: The recommendations in the OIG[2] model compliance programs are pretty good. The model suggests that the reporting system should be readily available and that there be the potential for anonymity. There should also be prompt study or investigation of any concern that is raised, and an effective and quick triage system to forward concerns that are not compliance related, such as human resources issues or informational concerns.

Troklus: Do you feel that outsourcing the hotline (reporting system) gives the system more credibility?

---

[2]Office of Inspector General

Bothe: No; credibility has a number of components. If an organization has to rely on outsourcing to provide credibility, perhaps it hasn't addressed some of the more fundamental issues: whether there is a serious commitment to compliance and whether there is trust regarding the anonymity and nonretaliation aspects. The more trust that exists in the institution overall, the more credibility will be lent to the reporting system.

Troklus: What steps can a compliance officer take to minimize the whistleblower threat?

Bothe: The lessons from other industries that have had to deal with whistleblowers are pretty compelling. There are fewer threats if there is a respected and well-publicized compliance program with a reputation for fair responses. Such a program becomes part of the informal information network within the institution. Employees know that issues called to the reporting system are going to be investigated, that the audit process is real, and that there is an effective feedback system to eliminate problems due to lack of education and errors. A good program creates a sense that the organization has an effective mechanism to deal with compliance issues. As long as issues brought to the attention of the organization are appropriately addressed, people won't feel that the only responsible action is to become a whistleblower.

Troklus: Who do you feel is responsible for conducting background checks: human resources, the compliance officer, or another unit?

Bothe: My own experience suggests that this needs to be joint, especially if the background checks form part of the employment application and ongoing employment record. The final documents and responsibility for obtaining them should sit where an employee's records are, e.g., in the human resources department. However, there are aspects of background checks that might not be well known to human resources personnel. The compliance professionals should be involved in the design of the background checking system and the follow-up of potential matches on sanction lists. When an institution is working under a corporate integrity agreement, the compliance officer is going to be the one who certifies that the sanction checking process has occurred. Background checks should not exist in an isolated fashion in one part of the organization.

Troklus: If an organization finds one of its physicians on the sanction list, what do you feel is the best way to handle the situation?

Bothe: Obviously, the first thing is to confirm that the name matches the individual. The action steps depend on the obligations of the institution. In general, corporate integrity agreements are quite explicit about this. These individuals cannot participate in any of the activities for which federal health care dollars are received. There is no option here. Once that match is identified, the required steps are discussed with the physician whose name is matched and the individuals to whom that physician reports.

Troklus: When noncompliance is identified in an institution, what are some effective forms of discipline?

Bothe: There are different kinds of noncompliance. Perhaps the largest category is lack of information. For this problem, the most appropriate step is education, perhaps on an individual tutorial basis, followed by early confirmation that the education had the desired effect. There are other categories of noncompliance that reflect a lack of priority in the individual's mind for the compliance effort. Creating that sense of priority is a shared responsibility and requires more effective communication to make compliance a priority for each individual. The final category—which I haven't yet encountered and suspect will be rare—is willful noncompliance. This requires clear due process that will not tolerate deviation from the institution's standards of compliance.

Troklus: What advice do you have for physicians considering an active role in compliance, such as being a compliance officer?

Bothe: A fundamental requirement is to know the regulations and the reasons why compliance is important. They need effective communication skills to be able to convey the rationale and imperatives for compliance to individuals both above and below them. They also need the real support of the organization to ensure that their responsibilities are going to be associated with the authority and the resources to carry out those responsibilities.

Troklus: Where do you see compliance in the next five years?

Bothe: Although it is not clear now, I think we'll have an agreed-upon set of billing guidelines and coding regulations, which will require constant education and reeducation efforts. Within the next five years, there will be more natural acceptance of compliance goals within organizations. We will have gotten over this cultural change, and it will become part of the fabric of the organization.

I think we have a challenge in the area of clinical research compliance. It will be a greater challenge in terms of information systems, integrating diverse financial reporting, better categorizing gray zones in standards of care, and determining what is covered under research protocols. We are just beginning the journey with clinical research compliance, and it will occupy our attention for the next three to five years as much as billing and coding have in the past three to five years.

Index

A

Academic medical center, 96–100, 167–174
  major compliance issues, 96, 168
Aging population, 143
Ambulance transport guidance, 3
American Health Information Management Association, 53
  coder certification, 57–58
  services, 53–54
ASAP line, 28
Audit, 159–160
  billing, 93
  concurrent, 163
  expansion, 164
  external audit, 161–162
  external firm, 160
  feedback to physicians, 162
  internal staff, 160
  monitoring, distinction, 160
  retrospective, 163
  risk matrix methodology, 163–164
  time frame, 107, 121, 131–132, 141, 160
Audit tool, 161

B

Background check, 172–173
  compliance officer, 25–26
  health care worker, database, 26
  nursing home worker, 25–26
Banking industry, regulation, 15
Billing, 64–82
  audit, 93
  monitoring, 152–153
  process, 55
Billing audit, 159–161
Billing error, fraud, differences, 77–78
Billing problem, long-term care, 21–22
Board of directors, 45, 102–103, 113–114, 128, 137, 154
  background, 45–46
  compliance program, 91–92
Budget
  commitment, 91, 151
  compliance, vi
  compliance program, 6–7, 151
  factors, 7

C

Certification, compliance officer, 92
Certified coding specialist, 53
Change management model, 170
Checklist, 45
Clinical assessment, accuracy, 21
Clinical justification, prospective payment system, 23

Clinical lab guidance, 2, 3–4
Code of conduct, hospital, 47
Coding, 37–38, 53–62
  accuracy, 168
  concurrent coding, 61
  conflicts between payer and coding system rules, 56–57
  continuing education, 60
  documentation, 54–56
  emergency room physician, 133
  frustrations, 54–55, 56–57
  monitoring, 152–153
  patient care issues, 61–62
  as profession, 58–59
  professional characteristics, 59–60
  settlement, 60–61
  severity of illness, 61–62
  training, 57, 58–59
Commitment, 129, 165
  budget, 91, 151
  compliance program, 70
  correlation with resources, 91
  physician, 39–40
Communication, corporate integrity agreement, 11–12
Compliance
  accomplishments, 47
  budget, vi
  business benefits, vi
  concept, 17
  defined, 65
  Department of Defense, 69–71
  difficult tasks, 48
  as enlightened self-interest, 124–125
  evolution, 149
  future, 41–42, 81–82, 99, 107, 121, 132–133, 155, 174
  growth and change, v
  Internet, 44–45
  key information, 39
  as major emphasis, 52
  most interesting activities, 44
  new issues, 107–108, 122–123, 133
  organizational culture, 141
  process, 55
  related fields or departments, 48–49
  resources, 44–45
Compliance committee, 103, 114–116, 128–129, 137, 151, 152
  physician, 168, 169
Compliance conference, 144
  government involvement, 145
Compliance consultant, compliance officer, transition, 33
Compliance counsel, 127
Compliance e-mail magazine, 107, 119–120, 131, 139
Compliance guidance, 1–2
  design process, 2
Compliance liaison, 164
Compliance listservs, 107, 119–120, 131, 139
Compliance officer, 17–29, 31–42
  advice for new, 42, 93–94, 155–156, 164–165
  authority, 151
  background, 17–18, 51, 83, 95–96, 153–154, 159
  background check, 25–26
  broadening, 89–91
  buy-in from physicians, 170
  as career, 28–29
  career path, 99
  certification, 92
  compliance consultant, transition, 33
  control, 151
  credentials, 25, 84–85
  criminal conduct, 13
  day-to-day challenges, 32–33
  experience, 25, 65–66, 84–85, 95–96, 101–102, 111–112, 135–136, 158–159
  history, 31–32

institutional review board, 99
interviewing employees, 89
liability, 12–13, 66–67
liability insurance, 67
mentor, 68
minimizing whistleblower threat, 172
nursing, 83–84
physician, 173–174
quality of care, 24, 83–84
research, 98–99
senior management, 66–67
sharing, 79–80
tenure, 31
training, monitoring, 38–39
as whistleblower, 108, 123–124, 133, 146
Compliance program
 benefits, 76
 board of directors, 91–92
 budget, 6–7, 151
  factors, 7
 commitment, 70
 effectiveness, 150
  elements, 87
  measurement, 87–89, 105, 117–118, 129–130, 138–139
 energy industry, 43–44
 evaluation, 7–8
 financial woes due to, 50–51
 future, 5–6
 implementation phase challenges, 41, 152–153
 measured effectiveness, 49
 medical billing company, 74–75
  effectiveness indicators, 75–76
  implementing, 80–81
 Montefiore Medical Center, 158
 Office of Inspector General
  draft compliance billing guidance, 71–73
  model guidance, 71

outcome-based measure, 7–8
physician support and involvement, 154–155
as prevention, 109
sanctions, 163
Sutter Health, 85–87
Vencor, 18–19
Compliance report, 103, 113–114, 128, 137, 154
Compliance web sites, 107, 119–120, 131, 139
Compliance Weekly, 119
Computer-based training, 104
Concurrent coding, 61
Confidentiality, 77
Conflict of interest, 96, 97
Consultant
 credibility, 68
 request for proposal, 151–152
 role, 67–69
 selection, 152
Continuing education. *See also* Training
 coding, 60
Corporate integrity agreement, 9–14, 172–173
 communication, 11–12
 extension, 10
 focus on individuals, 12
 future numbers, 13–14
 monitoring, 9–10
 numbers, 9
 organization responsibility, 12
 preparing in advance, 10–11
 problems or failures, 11
 sanctions, 173
Cost-based reimbursement, 21–22
Costs, 143
Credentialing, compliance officer, 84–85
Credibility, consultant, 68
Credit balance, 77

Criminal conduct, 12–13
  compliance officer, 13
  increasing amount, 14
  specific intent, 13

D

Department of Defense, compliance, 69–71
Department of Health and Human Services, Office of Inspector General, 1–15
Diagnostic related group audit, 122–123
Discipline, 173
  U.S. Sentencing Guidelines, 102, 112, 128, 136
Documentation
  coding, 54–56
  physician, 37–38
  prospective payment system, 23
Due diligence, 92

E

Effectiveness, 33–34
  defined, 87
  quantitative measures, 88–89
  standard, 89
Emergency room physician, coding, 133
Energy industry, compliance program, 43–44
Enforcement focus, 50
Error rate, 108
Ethical issues, 35, 135
  training, 120, 131, 138, 140
    senior management, 120–121, 131, 140–141
Evaluation, compliance program, 7–8

F

Federal Bureau of Investigation, 15
Flexible work schedule, 60
Fraud, billing error, differences, 77–78
Fraud and abuse, commercial payer, 106–107, 119, 130–131, 139
Fraud enforcement, 103

G

Go around compliance program, 54
Government Reform Committee, U.S. House of Representatives, 64

H

Health care
  crisis, 143
  financial perspective, 50–51
  trends, 153
Health care administration, concern about compliance, 150–151
Health Care Compliance Association, v, 25, 149
Health care corporate compliance. *See* Compliance
Health care worker, background check, database, 26
Health Insurance Portability and Accountability Act, 144
  privacy, 35
    official, 27
  privacy officer, 36
  reporting mechanisms, 27–28
Hospital, code of conduct, 47
Hospital utilization review director, 53
Hotline, 49
  marketing, 28
  outsourcing, 171–172

I

Implementation checklist, 45
Informed consent, 97
Institutional review board, compliance officer, 99
Internet, compliance, 44–45
Internet-based training, 138

L

Legal department, 91
Liability
 compliance officer, 12–13, 66–67
 senior management, 66–67
Liability insurance, compliance officer, 67
Litigation, 9, 111
Long-term care facility
 billing problem, 21–22
 training, 26
  mandatory *vs.* voluntary, 26–27
Long-Term Care Model Compliance Guide, 19–21

M

Managed hospital, 46–47
Management, resistance, 32–33
Medicaid, 21–22
Medical billing services, 64
 compliance program, 74–75
  effectiveness indicators, 75–76
  implementing, 80–81
  risk areas, 76–77
Medical school, compliance-related topics, 96–97
Medicare
 Final Rule for Teaching Physicians, 171
 nursing home system, 14–15
 Part A claims, 21
 Part B claims, 21

Mentor, compliance officer, 68
Monitoring
 auditing, distinction, 160
 billing, 152–153
 coding, 152–153
 corporate integrity agreement, 9–10
 feedback to physicians, 162
Montefiore Medical Center, 157
 compliance program, 158

N

National error rate, 108
National Institutes of Health, 4–5
Noncompliance, 173
Nursing, compliance officer, 83–84
Nursing home system
 chapter 11 bankruptcy, 14–15
 Medicare, 14–15
Nursing home worker, background check, 25–26

O

Office of Inspector General, 1–15
 assistant inspector general for legal affairs, 1–15
 guidances, 1–2
Organizational culture, compliance, 141
Outcome-based measure, compliance program, 7–8
Overutilization, 22
Owned hospital, 46–47

P

Patient care, 122
Physician
 commitment, 39–40
 compliance committee, 168, 169

compliance officer, 173–174
compliance program
  physicians' attitudes toward, 169–170
  support and involvement, 154–155
  documentation, 37–38
  role in compliance, 169
  sanction check, 40
    content, 40
  sanctions, 173
  training, 37–38
Physician guidance, 3
  third-party billing guidance, 73–74
Physicians at Teaching Hospitals, 5
Policies and procedures, 102, 112–113, 128, 136–157
  sharing of information, 168–169
  standardized, 47
Privacy, Health Insurance Portability and Accountability Act, 35
  official, 27
  privacy officer, 36
  reporting mechanisms, 27–28
Process audit, 159
Prospective payment system
  clinical justification, 23
  documentation, 23

Q

Quality of care, 23–24, 122, 133
  compliance officer, 24, 83–84
Quorum Health Resources, 43

R

Reengineering, 56
Refund, 107, 121, 131–132, 141

Registered health information administrator, 53
Regulation
  banking industry, 15
  complexity, 56, 106, 118–119, 144, 145–146
  frustration, 105–106, 118, 130, 145–146
  simplification, 144, 146
Reporting mechanism, 171
  anonymous, 49, 103, 116, 129, 137–138
  outsourcing, 171–172
Request for proposal
  components, 151–152
  consultant, 151–152
Research, 97
  compliance, 4–5
  compliance officer, 98–99
  penalties and sanctions, 98
Resource Utilization Group, 21
Risk management department, 90–91
RUGs creep, 22

S

Sanction check, 14
  physician, 40
    content, 40
Sanctions
  compliance program, 163
  physician, 173
Self-disclosure, 149, 153, 171
Senior management, 137
  commitment, 28–29
  compliance officer, 66–67
  liability, 66–67
Settlement, 149
  coding, 60–61
  money recovered, 14
  reasons for, 8–9

Standard, effectiveness, 89
Statute of limitations, 77, 107
Sutter Health, compliance program, 85–87
Systems thinking, 45

T

Third-party billing guidance, physician practice guidance, 73–74
Training, 32, 104, 117, 129, 138–139, 152
   across the board training, 34
   annual compliance education, 96
   challenges for compliance officers, 36–37
   coding, 57, 58–59
   compliance officer, monitoring, 38–39
   computer-based training, 104
   ethical issues, 120, 131, 140
      senior management, 120–121, 131, 140–141
   focus areas, 34–35
   hours of training, 34
   in-house *vs.* external, 36
   inservice session, 104
   interactive, 129
   internal education processes, 150
   Internet-based training, 138
   long-term care facility, 26
      mandatory *vs.* voluntary, 26–27
   mandatory *vs.* voluntary, 34
   physician, 37–38
   pre- and posttests, 38
   two-tiered educational process, 162–163

U

Underutilization, 22–23
University of Chicago, structure, 167
University of Pennsylvania, 96
U.S. Sentencing Guidelines, discipline, 102, 112, 128, 136
Utilization, incentives to providers to control, 22–23

V

Vencor
   compliance program, 18–19
   current compliance initiatives, 19
   organizational structure, 18
Voluntary disclosure, 78–79

W

Working at home, 60